THOSE WHO
REMAIN

by

Charles R. Taylor, D.D.
President
Today In Bible Prophecy, Inc.

Published by

Today In Bible Prophecy, Inc.

Printed by
Europa Graphics
Santa Ana, Calif.

DEDICATED

To the glory of God!

    With special appreciation to my faithful wife, Virginia, who has sacrificed much for my ministry of research and writing.

TABLE OF CONTENTS

FOREWORD

"As it was in the days of Noah, even so shall it be also in the days of the Son of Man. They ate, they drank, they married, they were given in marriage until THE DAY!"

Christians who are looking for the return of the Lord will thrill at the contents of this remarkable book.

Multitudes in all parts of the world have expressed their approval of Dr. Taylor's straightforwardness and sound doctrine.

It is written in a style so plain, so fascinating that young and old, saved or unsaved, will read it with almost breathless interest from start to finish.

Many thousands who would never have studied their Bibles or looked at an ordinary book to learn the precious truths of the Second Coming of the Lord, have been awakened, quickened and even converted by reading Dr. Taylor's books on prophecy, namely: *World War III and the Destiny of America* and the smaller edition, *The Destiny of America*, followed closely by the best seller, *Get All Excited Jesus Is Coming Soon.* Each in turn was convincingly true, beautiful and startling in the annals of Christian literature.

Dr. Taylor's latest book, *Those Who Remain,* is destined to bless and thrill those looking for the Lord's return. It will awaken careless, ill-taught Christians to a complete realization of the fact that the coming of the Lord draweth nigh.

I have known Dr. Charles Taylor for more than thirty-five years and highly esteem the privilege of introducing his latest book, *Those Who Remain.*

He has been a prophetic scholar, teacher and preacher for forty years. With keen acumen and trained scholarship, he has proclaimed Scriptures seemingly hidden to the casual student and those not given to deep study and meditation of the Word.

Not all can be specialists in this field. Dr. Taylor has shown his fitness for the calling, and he has in this contribution put into concrete form, simple for all to comprehend, the theme of the Second Coming. He has given us a guide of the mystifying intricacies in theological thinking. He does not merely express opinions, but takes the facts as presented by the Word of God.*

I recommend this book, *Those Who Remain,* to those who are beginning the subject. I am sure it will be as much of a blessing to others as it has been to me.

J. Leonard Bell

J. Leonard Bell B.D., D.D., Th.D.
President, World Missions Far Corners

---

* Although he points out time factors and great potentials developing now he does not set dates, nor is he dogmatic.

INTRODUCTION

This message is an extremely important one. It is intended for THOSE WHO REMAIN after the holocaust of World War III.

The world already is preparing for the coming holocaust, a terrible battle by fire prophesied in the Bible. The book of Revelation prophesies that one-third of the Earth will be burned and greatly devastated by this war, which we commonly call World War III. It also prophesies that one-fourth of the people of Earth will be killed. The nuclear exchange will only last for one day (several of the prophecies verify this), but the effects of it will last for nearly seven years, the Bible says.

The United States of America faces its greatest danger since the revolution of 1776 brought it into being. American cities soon will burn. But this great nation will survive.

THOSE WHO REMAIN is designed to give guidance and help to the innocent bystanders and survivors of the coming Russian nuclear attack prophesied in so many places in the Bible.

Evangelical churches will not be functioning at that time, for an event called "the rapture of the Church" will take place just before World War III. Those missing will have been translated (transported) to Heaven in a moment, "in the twinkling of an eye," as prophesied in the Scriptures.[1]

The many documentations in this book give solid evidence that the *rapture of the Church* and God's judgment on Earth are both very, very near.

The Lord has given us many prophecies about *the signs of the times* and His return. Now, those prophecies are coming to pass, and His return is not only imminent: it is at the very doors.

Whatever you intend to do or hope to do for Christ, you need to do it *now.*

Thousands of books have been written about the Bible and the return of Christ, but most have been written in very general terms. His return is so near as I write this book that much *specific* information has been included. The Christian world needs to be "on the alert."

Jesus Christ our Lord said,

> **"And when these things *begin* to come to pass, then look up, and lift up your heads; for your redemption draweth nigh" (Luke 21:28).**

This is the sixth book I have written. The contents of the first two were included in my third and major book *World War III and the Destiny of America.* That book was later condensed to a pocket edition called *The Destiny of America.* But more specific information was needed.

Bible prophecy was being fulfilled in greater measure day by day, and I had accumulated specific news items and articles in documentary form over a considerable period of time. I compared these news items with the Scriptures and again began to write.

As time seemed to draw so near for the return of Christ, I wrote *Get All Excited — Jesus Is Coming Soon.* The evidence I presented caused such excitement among Christians that thousands of souls were led to a saving knowledge of Christ. People bought the books by the tens and fifties to send to their friends and relatives around the world. The message of warning and of salvation was having its effect. Christians were being stirred into activity and many souls were being born-again into the eternal family of God.

Because the book pointed strongly to the *potential* for our Lord's return in 1975 (even though the Lord's coming in that year was not predicted in the book), some people lost their zeal by the end of the year. An attitude of lethargy and luke-warmness seemed to set in.

Updated Information

This new book has been prepared to update and extend the news about our Lord's return and to stimulate hearts and lives anew into activity and into dedicated service for our Lord until the very moment when Jesus comes for His own.

Before He left this world to ascend into Heaven, Jesus gave the Great Commission:

"Go ye into all the world and preach the Gospel to every creature" (Mark 16:15).

Christ knew that they would not and could not go in their own strength. On the day that He ascended, therefore, He gave them a solemn promise:

"Ye shall receive power, *after that the Holy Ghost is come upon you;* and ye shall be witnesses unto me both in Judea, and in Samaria, and unto the uttermost part of the Earth" (Acts 1:8).

Now, in these last days, God is pouring out His Holy Spirit in greater measure than at any time since the initial baptism with the Holy Spirit on the prophesied Feast of Weeks, the day of Pentecost. Christians are being filled to overflowing, and thousands of God's people are fervently witnessing for Christ at every opportunity. I praise God for this.

THOSE WHO REMAIN is a summary of news and information diligently compared with the Bible so you can become a more effective servant of the Lord. This book gives specific evidences that you can use in telling others about the return of the Lord.

Also, this book verifies that the *rapture of the Church* will occur very soon.

Let's not become victims of Laodicean lethargy and self-indulgence. Let's go everywhere with the message of Christ. Let's use the telephone to tell others about Jesus and His great saving power. We have very little time left to serve the Lord of Glory!

For THOSE WHO REMAIN, this book will give spiritual guidance and practical suggestions on *how to survive* during the seven-year era called "the Tribulation period."

Read with care. Your life could depend on it.

Footnotes

[1] I Cor. 15:51-57 and I Thess. 4:13-18.

"In a moment, in the twinkling of an eye . . ."

CHAPTER 1

MILLIONS MISSING

Millions of people soon are going to disappear from this planet.

The event is called the *rapture of the Church* when "the Lord himself shall descend from heaven with a shout, the voice of the archangel, and the trump of God; and the dead in Christ shall rise first: then we who are alive and remain (at that moment) shall be *caught up* together with them in the clouds, *to meet the Lord in the air*" (I Thess. 4:16, 17).

When the *rapture* takes place, adults who truly believe in Jesus Christ (and also the millions of innocent babies and young children throughout the world) will be taken to heaven "in a moment, in the twinkling of an eye" (I Cor. 15:51-53).

Chaos

The world will be plunged into chaos. THOSE WHO REMAIN will be in a state of shock. They will be awe-stricken, fearful and trembling.

I can only briefly describe here some of the chaos the world will experience:

People will be missing from all walks of life.

Airplanes will veer off their courses and many will crash because their Christian pilots and co-pilots will have been *caught up* to be with the Lord.

Trains will run wild, and many will crash, as Christian switchmen and engineers vanish.

The world's highways will be a tangle of wrecks because many, many thousands of Christian drivers will have disappeared. The dazed, fearful and astonished survivors of these crashes will grope through the debris looking for their loved ones; but they won't find them. They will have been taken bodily to Heaven in a split second.

All communication lines will be jammed as THOSE WHO REMAIN search for those who have disappeared.

Police, fire and rescue crews will work around the clock. Hospitals will overflow. Emergency shelters and first aid stations will be inadequate. The Red Cross and all other emergency units, plus the military facilities, still will not be enough.

Emergency governmental powers will be put into effect to stop looting, killing and fighting over the spoils that those who have gone will have left behind. Insurrectionists will become opportunists. Anarchy will prevail in many areas. Governments will quake and tumble as the established order is shaken to the core.

Effect to be Worldwide

Multitudes will be missing, in greater or lesser degree, all over the Earth. Wherever there were true believers in Jesus, people will be missing — in America, China, Asia, the islands of the seas, South Africa; all over the world.

More will be missing from the predominantly Christian countries. But even there, vast multitudes will be left behind. Even the most godly countries are not godly any more. *This is the reason God will remove His own people: so He can bring trial and tribulation on THOSE WHO REMAIN to see if they will repent and turn to Him for salvation.*

"As I live, saith the Lord God, I have no pleasure in the death of the wicked; but that the wicked turn from his way and live" (Ezek. 33:11).

God wants YOU to turn from your wild dash after pleasure, lust and sin; He wants you to seek the way of eternal life. HE WANTS TO SAVE YOU.

The Bible says this will be a time of great fear and stress declaring that "men's hearts shall fail them, for fear of the things which are coming to pass on the earth" (Luke 21:26).

Don't Believe 'Official Explanation'

Authorities will try to explain the disappearances. Science fiction writers today are pre-conditioning the minds of the masses to the point they will believe anything — even that a vast armada of UFOs came swiftly and suddenly, snatching millions out of the world. But don't fall for these imaginations. Don't believe the great lie that the news media will spread as the official explanation.

No UFO armada will be needed. No invasion from outer space by some weird creatures will be responsible for the disappearances.

The saints of God and all the innocent babies will have been instantly carried into Heaven by the power of God — a phenomenon similar to the resurrection and ascension of Jesus. They will enter into heaven to abide in peace and splendor forever.

A Man of Great Power

Out of the stress and turmoil will step a man of great power who will claim to have all the answers. His coming is prophesied in the Bible, which declares he will come forth "with all power and signs and lying wonders."

DON'T BELIEVE THIS MAN. DON'T FOLLOW HIM! He will be the one referred to in the Bible as *the beast*; the one commonly called *the Antichrist*.

When these things happen, the Tribulation period will have begun. The Bible says it will last for seven years. It will be *a time of judgment* and of great distress on Earth as God pours out judgment after judgment to cause mankind to consider his ways and to look to Him for deliverance.

CHAPTER 2

THE ANTICHRIST

While the world is in its initial turmoil, Russia will mobilize its huge armies and prepare to advance against the Middle East crossroads nation of Israel.

This is predicted in Ezek. 38:10-12:

> "Thus saith the Lord God: It shall also come to pass that at the same time things shall come into thy mind, and thou shalt think an evil thought: And thou shalt say, I will go up to the land of unwalled villages (Kibbutzim); I will go to them that are at rest, that dwell safely, all of them dwelling without walls, and having neither bars nor gates, to take a spoil, and to take a prey; to turn thine hand upon the desolate places that are now inhabited, and UPON THE PEOPLE THAT ARE GATHERED OUT OF THE NATIONS, which have gotten cattle and goods, that dwell in the midst of the land."

As Russia prepares its mighty armies and its great armada of ships, Israel desperately will seek a positive guarantee of protection and a guarantee of its borders.

The Geneva Middle East peace conference will probably be called back into session in a crash effort to seek a solution that might avert World War III.

Bible prophecy will be fulfilled again when the prominent leader with the miracle-working power finally guarantees Israel's security with a seven-year treaty (Dan. 9:27).

Before we continue with the sequence of events after the *rapture of the Church*, let's examine some prophecies about the Antichrist.

Prophecies About the Antichrist

Nearly 2,000 years ago, Jesus warned His generation about the coming of the false leader.

"I am come in my Father's name and ye receive me not,"

He said. "If another shall come in his own name, him ye will receive" (John 5:43).

In the sixth Century B.C., the prophet Daniel wrote:

> "And the king shall do according to his will; and he shall exalt himself, and magnify himself . . . and shall prosper till the indignation be accomplished: for that that is determined shall be done" (Dan. 11:36).

The Apostle Paul wrote:

> "And then shall that Wicked One be revealed . . . even him, whose coming is after the working of Satan with all power and signs and lying wonders, and with all deceivableness of unrighteousness in them that perish; because they received not the love of the truth, that they might be saved" (II Thess. 2:8-10).

In the Book of Revelation, this man of sin, called the Antichrist and "the king," is referred to as "the beast:"

> "And the ten horns which you saw are ten kings, which have received no kingdom as yet; but receive power as kings one hour with *the beast*. These shall have one mind, and shall give their power and strength unto *the beast*" (Rev. 17:12, 13).

Daniel 11:39 says, "And he shall cause them to rule over many, and shall divide the land for gain."

All these Scriptural references, and many more, point to the fact that a strong king is coming who will have "all power and signs and lying wonders."

He will be the leader of the ten-nation entity that other Scripture references identify as the Western European area of the old Roman Empire. He will befriend Israel and will guarantee its protection for seven years. His time of rule will be during the "latter days," commonly called the *Tribulation period*. That time begins immediately after the *rapture of the Church*.

It is *after* Bible-believing Christians are taken out of this world that the Wicked One, the Antichrist, will be revealed and perform those things prophesied about his dominion.

When that man of destiny, the military leader of Western Europe, is making his boasts about bringing peace to Israel, therefore, or that he will destroy the Russian and Arab armies that threaten Israel, the Tribulation period will have begun.

The ten-nation entity over which the Antichrist will rule will be the outgrowth of the present Common Market of Western Europe. He will be considered a military genius and will prove himself by entering into conflict with the Russians and Arabs when they strike in force against Israel.

According to specific Bible prophecy, the Russians and Arabs are destined to defeat, and the Antichrist will claim the victory. As a result, he will gain full control of the region formerly held by the Roman legions. He will, according to Dan.11:44, go forth "with great fury" and conquer even more territory, becoming a world ruler.

The United States of America will suffer much as a prime target of the Russians in their great nuclear attack. But while America will be allied with the Antichrist for World War III, it will not likely come under the total jurisdiction of that man of destiny. The leaders of the 10 Western European nations, however, will be so greatly impressed by the Antichrist's wonders and solutions that they "shall give their power and strength unto the beast" (Rev. 17:13). In the process, he will uproot three of the original 10 rulers and will replace them with three of his own choosing, thus dividing the land "for gain" (Dan. 7:8 and 11:39).

Warning

Let me repeat my warning: *Do not* follow after that military leader. He is called "Antichrist" because he is contrary to Christ. He will ultimately command all people to worship himself as God.

He also will require all people to receive an identification mark, which the Bible calls "the mark of the beast" or the number of his name (666). No person will be allowed to buy or sell unless he has the identification mark inscribed on his forehead or hand. Is it possible? Note the following:

Dec. 1977, RADAR NEWS: "Mr. F. Paul Peterson reports contacting IBM personnel and university professors who were knowledgeable about computers. He reports, 'They all agreed (1) that it is possible with present technology to computerize the whole world, (2) that there does exist a laser invisible tattoo mark that can be put on the back of the hand and on the forehead, (3) that there is a scanner, when passed over the hand, that can connect immediately with a person's bank account, and wherever a person purchases anything, the amount can be deducted and no checks or money are needed, (4) that there are supermarkets in some American cities which already are experimenting with such computers.''

Yes, the technology already is here and becoming more prevalent in use every day. When the time comes for Satan's man to require the identifying "mark of the beast," it will be enforceable. To receive the mark, however, each person will be required to bow down and worship the man or his image.

If you are among THOSE WHO REMAIN, read carefully God's declaration concerning those who worship that devil-possessed man:

"If any man worship the beast and his image, and receive his mark in his forehead, or in his hand, the same shall drink of the wine of the wrath of God, which is poured out without mixture into the cup of his indignation; and he shall be tormented with fire and brimstone in the presence of the holy angels, and in the presence of the Lamb; and the smoke of their torment ascendeth up for ever and ever: and they have no rest day or night, who worship the beast and his image, and whosoever receiveth the mark of his name" (Rev. 14:9-11).

Any person who takes the mark of Satan's man steps outside the redemption of Christ. There is *no* salvation for that person because taking the mark of the beast is a rejection of the salvation provided in Jesus Christ the Lord.

CHAPTER 3

PREPARATIONS FOR WORLD WAR III

War clouds are looming on the horizon.

Nearly every one of the prophets of the Bible wrote about a great battle by fire. John described it extensively in Revelation 8, and now we recognize that as a prophecy concerning a thermonuclear war.

Millions will die in the holocaust, which will effect one-third of the world; and millions more will suffer and die from post-war devastations and supernatural judgments. More on this later.

Alignment of Nations

The Bible identifies the exact nations and areas that will be involved in this holocaust.[1] I have listed each of these countries by its ancient Bible name and by its modern name in my book *World War III and the Destiny of America*.[2]

All of Eastern Europe (except Greece) and all of the Arab nations will fight against Israel. All of Western Europe and the United States will defend it. The Soviet Union, the Warsaw Pact nations and the Arabs united in attack, will suffer dire defeat. And the military leader of Western Europe will claim the victory.

The Warsaw Pact nations *already* are aligned with the Arabs. And the United States (backed by the Western European powers) is now negotiating on behalf of Israel. It is evident, therefore, that Bible prophecies about the great conflict are about to come to pass.

This being so, the Antichrist *must* be alive somewhere, ready to be launched into his position as the military leader of Western Europe.

The Bible says his identity will not be revealed until immediately after the *rapture of the Church*. But there is a man today who seems to have all the Bible-required qualifications.

King Juan Carlos de Borbon

Juan Carlos de Borbon I, King of Spain, is a direct descendant of the kings of Spain, of France and England. He was born in Rome, Italy, on January 5, 1938. He spent his early years in Italy and in Switzerland, but in 1948 (the year Israel became a nation) his father met with Generalissimo Francisco Franco on the Portuguese border and agreed that Juan Carlos should be educated in Spain in preparation for the monarchy. His father, Don Carlos, remained in self-imposed exile in Portugal.

In 1945, Don Juan, pretender to the throne of Spain, sent a manifesto to Franco suggesting that he resign. Two years later the Law of Succession to the Throne was adopted. Article 13 of that law stated:

"The head of state . . . may propose to the Cortes that there be excluded from succession those royal persons . . . who, because of their acts, deserve to lose the rights of succession established in this law."

In December 1954, Don Juan acknowledged his rejection and agreed with Franco that Juan Carlos, then 16, should be the presumptive heir.

On July 23, 1969, Generalissimo Francisco Franco stood before a full session of the Spanish Cortes (Parliament) and declared:

"The relief of the Chief of State is a normal act imposed by man's mortality. Conscious of my responsibility before God and history, I have decided to recommend Prince Juan Carlos de Borbon y Borbon as my successor."

The next day, Franco returned to the Cortes, this time with Prince Juan Carlos, who was dressed in the uniform of an army captain. Juan Carlos had come to take the oath of office and of loyalty to the existing regime. He was asked:

"Do you in the name of God and the Holy Gospels swear loyalty to his excellency the Chief of State and the principles of the National Movement and the fundamental laws of Spain?"

"Yes, I do so swear," he replied.

Some of the wording of his acceptance speech reveals ambition and thoughts of grandeur. He said:

> **"I AM FULLY CONSCIOUS OF THE RESPON-
> SIBILITIES I AM ASSUMING . . . I WANT TO SERVE
> my nation publicly, and for our people, I WANT
> PROGRESS, DEVELOPMENT, UNITY, JUSTICE,
> LIBERTY AND *GRANDEUR* . . ."**

I can not and do not say King of Spain Juan Carlos I will definitely become the prophesied Antichrist, but I do note his qualifications. He has the military training, is a descendant of the kings of three Western European nations and was born in Rome, the heart of the Old Roman Empire. He is tall (6' 3"), handsome and highly regarded. More important, he is liked by the army and the powerful Civil Guard of Spain. His rule will certainly be backed by military power.

King of Jerusalem

Spain's consul general in Jerusalem is Santiago de Churruca Plaza. He is of Spanish nobility, having the title Count de Campo Rey.

In November 1975, when Juan Carlos became king, Count de Campo Rey said the swearing in of Prince Juan Carlos de Borbon as King of Spain automatically revived an ancient title applied to Spanish monarchs, "KING OF JERU-SALEM."

He said the title, hereditary in Spanish royalty since the Middle Ages "while empty and merely honorific," today is nevertheless "extremely precious." He said that "Catholic Kings" of Spain had been recognized by Popes and by Muslim rulers for centuries as "protectors of Catholic Holy Land interests," and that, although Spanish influence was later superseded partially by French, "certain sites and monasteries in the Holy Land" are still *under Spanish protection.*

Could this only be coincidental, coming at this time in history?

Juan Carlos was a prince in training for 27 years (1948-1975). Bible prophecy specifies, "The *prince* who shall come" (Dan. 9:26).

The prophesied *man of sin* mentioned in Revelation 13 and 17 as *the beast* and commonly called *the Antichrist*, is associated with Rome (Rev. 17:9, 18). Juan Carlos was born in Rome. He has always been a Roman Catholic and is reportedly a member of the Spanish-founded Sacerdotal Society of Holy Cross and Opus Dei,[3] a Roman Catholic religious order of men, which has its international headquarters in Rome.

In his vision of the terrible beast, recorded in Daniel 7, that prophet saw a "little horn" come up on the head of this beast "among" ten original horns. The little horn then "plucked up by the roots" three of the original horns.

Spain is not a member of the Common Market, but is coming up "among" those nations. Juan Carlos is being more readily accepted day by day. If he becomes a strong ruler who displays military genius, it is very likely that all of Western Europe will honor him, for there has been no military strong man in the Common Market region since the days of Gen. Charles de Gaulle, former President of France.

Juan Carlos became the king of Spain after 27 years of special training. He is a graduate of Spain's Naval Academy, its Air Force Academy and of the Saragosa Military Academy, where he was graduated third in a class of 271.

He also has had diplomatic training and has served in various governmental capacities.

At the ceremonies in his honor following his inauguration, he wore the uniform of Captain General, the highest rank in the Spanish military organization.

He is the reigning King of Spain, King of Jerusalem.

He *might* become the King of Europe, the Antichrist.

Juan Carlo's wife, Queen Sophia, is daughter of King Paul and Queen Frederica of Greece. Her brother is exiled King Constantine. She represents a branch on a geneological tree that includes two German emperors, 18 kings of Denmark, five kings of Sweden, seven emperors of Russia, a king and a queen of Norway, a queen of England and five kings of Greece.

Juan Carlos is descended from the many kings of Spain, of

the Bourbon dynasty of France and of the kings of England. He is the cousin of Queen Elizabeth II of Britain and a great-grandson of the renowned Queen Victoria. His training for the position of King of Spain included much diplomatic training and extensive military preparation. In the course of it he mastered five languages of Europe, and he has been guest of honor in the courts of leading countries.

Two Other Potential Kings

In spite of the many, many qualifications that seem to identify King Juan Carlos I as the man with the potential for becoming the prophesied Antichrist, I must be faithful to reveal some evidence that could point to one or two other possible kings.

King Alphonso XIII reigned as King of Spain from 1886 to 1931. He was king when the civil war broke out that deposed him and brought Gen. Francisco Franco into power as the victorious dictator.

While still king, Alphonso had named as his regent — his successor — a nephew by the name of Francis Xavier. Xavier's son is Prince Carlos Hugo Bourbon-Parma, and there is an organized minority in Spain known as "the Carlists" who support this prince-designate for the monarchy.

Prince Carlos de Bourbon-Parma is a friend of leftists in Spain who oppose the post-Franco rightist regime of King Juan Carlos I. But perhaps even more significant is the fact that Carlist pretender Prince Carlos de Bourbon-Parma is married to the daughter of Prince Bernhard of The Netherlands, one of the wealthiest men in the world. He is well known as chairman of the Bilderberger international banking combine that has as its apparent goal the establishment of a one-world government. This makes the pretender prince a possibility for succession to the Spanish throne if something should happen to King Juan Carlos I. It could put a puppet king in position to be used by the very powerful Bilderberger international bankers.

Because of this association with the extremely wealthy and powerful banking group, Prince Carlos de Bourbon-Parma can be considered a potential candidate for becoming the Antichrist.

But since he has strong leftist (communist) associations, and one of his closest friends is Norodom Sihanouk, the one who paved the way for red terror in Cambodia, I don't believe he could become the Antichrist king. According to Bible prophecy, the Antichrist will be a king of the free Western European nations, and he is destined to fight *against* the communist bloc of nations in World War III.

While Prince Carlos de Bourbon-Parma is a friend of the Communists, King Juan Carlos de Borbon y Borbon is a longtime opponent of any form of communism.

Don Carlos

Don Carlos, father of King Juan Carlos I and a proCommunist, is supported in his bid for the monarchy by the Democratic Junta. The Junta is dominated by Santiago Carillos, secretary-general of the Spanish Communist Party. For this reason, therefore, although he could become the future king, I think he is an unlikely person to become the Antichrist. Generalissimo Francisco Franco, a staunch antiCommunist, refused to even consider Don Juan as a possible successor to the Spanish throne, by-passing him in favor of his son Juan Carlos.

Today Juan Carlos de Borbon y Borbon reigns as King Juan Carlos I, King of Spain, King of Jerusalem. With his command of European languages, with his extensive diplomatic, air force, navy and army training — which puts him in high esteem by the very powerful Spanish Civil Guard — because he holds the position of Captain General, the highest military position in the Spanish army; and because he was born in Rome and received his lifelong training in the Roman Catholic Sacerdotal Society of the Holy Cross and Opus Dei, I consider him the most likely person alive to become the prophesied infamous Antichrist.

Warning Signals

The *first warning* that the Antichrist is assuming his great authority will be a manifestation of his miracle-working power — whether that man is Juan Carlos or someone else.

II Thess. 2:9 says the revelation of the man called the Antichrist will be *"after the working of Satan with all power and signs and lying wonders."* Expect this to happen!

The *second warning* will be his definite move to "confirm the covenant with many" Israelis, guaranteeing their security.

The miracle-working Antichrist will become the military leader of the ten-nation Western European empire in "one hour." The actual time will probably be two weeks, based on the fact that the seven-year Tribulation era is referred to as "one week" in Scripture.

It represents one week of years. If one "week" is seven years, then one "day" would be one year. Since there are 24 hours in a day, "one hour" would therefore be 1/24th of one year, which equals one-half of one month — about two weeks of actual time.

Rev. 17:12 says that the ten rulers of Western Europe will rule "one hour with the beast" and that they will "have one mind, and will give their power and strength unto the beast." They will accept his leadership and his rule over them. When that happens, he will have the authority to guarantee Israel's security from a position of strength.

When the Antichrist personally guarantees Israel's security — and most likely authorizes Israel's control of the temple site, which now houses the Islamic Mosque of Omar (the Dome of the Rock) — it will greatly infuriate the Arabs.

They will attack Israel in force, this time backed by the military and strategic might of the U.S.S.R., and World War III will be the result.

Nuclear Fury

Knowing that it will have to fight the defenders of Israel, the United States of America and Western Europe, Russia will undoubtedly strike furiously at the United States and the NATO nations simultaneously with its attack against Israel. Because of the world's turmoil, caused by the disappearance of millions of people in *the rapture*, these nations will be upset and unprepared — but not so much that their milli-second phase-array radar and other automated defense mechanisms cannot be activated. The computerized response of the Western powers to the Russian attack will be colossal and horrendous. It is recorded in Ezek. 39:4.

> "And I will send a fire on the land of Magog (Russia) and among those that dwell carelessly in the coastlands."

The war will be reciprocal. Russia will blast the Western nations, and the Western countries will rain nuclear death and destruction on Russia.

Russia is never mentioned again as a nation after World War III. It is prophesied, however, that America will be a nation even during the millenial reign of our Lord Jesus Christ. America will bring its present "to the place of the name of the Lord of hosts, the mount Zion" (Isa. 18:7). Zechariah says this will be done "year by year." America will survive!

World War III *is* prophesied. It is destined to happen at the very beginning of the Tribulation period.

If the great one-day thermonuclear war (Ezek. 39:6-8) was not scheduled to occur at the *beginning* of the seven-year Tribulation, then robbery of the fallen (Ezek. 39:9, 10) would extend into the millenial reign of Christ, which would be contrary to all prophecies about the bliss of that era.

One-Third of the Earth

One of the most amazing documentations in the book *World War III and the Destiny of America* is that in A.D. 95 the Apostle John (Rev. 8:1-12) wrote that one-third of all trees will be burned up; one-third of the world's ships will be destroyed; one-third of the Earth's fresh waters will become bitter (radioactive), causing people to die; and one-third of the sky will be blackened by (probably atomic) clouds.

In other words, ONE-THIRD OF THE WORLD will be involved in World War III.

In *World War III and the Destiny of America* I tabulate by country, region and association the specific land areas that will be involved. The amazing part of this documentation is that the total of the land mass of those countries specifically referred to in the Bible comes to exactly one-third of the total land areas of the world. God's Word always verifies God's Word!

For the complete documentation and tabulation of the names and land areas of the countries to be involved in World War III, according to the specific prophecies of the Bible, write for *World War III and the Destiny of America*. See the last page of this book for ordering details.

Preparations Underway

In 1972 the United Nations reported that the world's nuclear arsenals contain enough explosives to blast every man, woman and child on Earth with the equivalent of 15 tons of TNT. The past several years has seen great development in delivery systems and in the accuracy of those systems.

Missiles now can be fired many thousands of miles and strike within a few feet of the intended target. Technology has increased tremendously. Cruise missiles, for example, fired from small missile ships, from submarines or dropped from bombers can pinpoint land on targets 2,500 miles down-range over water or rough terrain. A Boeing 747 could launch as many as 100 of them. Their flight is under radar range, for they cruise at altitudes of less than 200 feet, making them very formidable weapons. They carry either conventional or nuclear warheads.

The superpowers are in a race in technology, research and development. Fortunately the United States is way ahead in this field; but the Russians are catching up fast.

An Oct. 4, 1974 Associated Press dispatch from Washington states: "The Soviet Union has test-fired two new long-range, submarine-launched missiles about 4,900 miles from the far north Barents Sea into the Pacific, the Pentagon announced Thursday."

Those missiles are now operational, classified as 4,200-mile missiles. This was reported in an Associated Press (AP) article from London, printed in The Los Angeles Times, Jan. 3, 1976. That article reads, in part, "Russia's submarines, with their 4,200-mile missiles, could hit 'pretty well the whole of North

America, Europe and a pretty large hunk of China' without leaving the Barents Sea off their Arctic coast, says Capt. John Moore in his authoritative book, *The Soviet Navy Today*.

"In surface ships, Moore says, the Russians' new Kara class guided-missile cruiser, at 10,000 tons with surface-to-surface and surface-to-air missiles, is more formidable than the 14,500-ton Little Rock, flagship of the U.S. 6th Fleet in the Mediterranean that carries only surface-to-air missiles.

"He declares, 'The Soviet navy has become the most potent in fire-power of any fleet that ever existed . . . far more powerful than needed for defense.' And Russia has more submarines than all of the NATO countries combined, including the United States."

Russia has more intercontinental ballistic missiles than does the United States and it has larger nuclear warheads on them. We do have more total warheads, however, because we developed the MIRV multiple-warhead missiles before Russia did. The United States has over 7,000 nuclear weapons in the NATO countries of Western Europe besides thousands of missiles in continental U.S. and in our Polaris and Poseidon nuclear submarines. *Both superpowers are super-armed!*

Strategically, Russia, Eastern Europe (Warsaw Pact nations) and the Arab countries are all aligned *against the nation of Israel*, exactly as prophesied by Ezekiel and Daniel nearly 600 years before Christ. Conversely, the nations of Western Europe (including Greece) and the United States of America are aligned *in defense of Israel*. Confrontation is imminent, and the Bible declares that *a great war will happen*.

At the Time of the End

Dan. 11:40 declares,

> "And at the time of the end shall the king of the south push at him: and the king of the north shall come against him like a whirlwind, with chariots (tanks), and with horsemen, and *with many ships* . . ."

Right after the Antichrist guarantees the security of Israel, note that "the king of the south," representing the Arabs, and "the king of the north," representing the Soviets, are depicted as striking "at him," the Antichrist king. The next verse says "he shall enter also into the glorious land," obstensibly to protect it from the invaders from the south and the north. Verse 42 specifies that "Egypt shall not escape." Egypt and the other Arab lands, except for Jordan that will be taken by Israel, will all fall into the hands of the Antichrist.

In this prophecy, Russia is depicted as coming "with many ships." Not until fifteen years ago did Russia have enough ships to even talk about. Today it has the largest navy in the world.

Bible prophecy is being fulfilled, and the time for World War III is almost at hand.

The Victor

The Antichrist will be the acclaimed victor of World War III. Dan. 11:42 says he will overthrow many countries "and the land of Egypt shall not escape." By conquest he will be the undisputed ruler of all the old Roman Empire. His end-time rule will be greatly expanded, and he will then "go forth with great fury to destroy . . ." (Dan. 11:44).

The Antichrist will not be a man of peace as some seek to portray. He only makes a covenant of peace with Israel when he guarantees Israel's security.

He wants Israel to prosper because "in the midst of the week" (after 3½ years of his seven-year treaty) he will cause the sacrifices at the rebuilt temple in Jerusalem to cease. He will at that time declare himself to be God, "sitting in the temple of God, showing himself that he is God" (II Thess. 2:4). When this happens, the most severe of God's tribulation judgments will fall upon mankind. So great will be the punishments that God will pour out in those days, that it will be as Jesus prophesied in Matt. 24:21, 22:

"For then shall be great tribulation, such as was not since the beginning of the world to this time, no nor ever shall be. And except those days should be shortened there should no flesh be saved: but for the elect's sake those days shall be shortened."

The Truth of This Message

The first proof of the truth of this message will be the great airlift of the true Christians and of all infants into Heaven "in a moment, in the twinkling of an eye." The Bible says, "The Lord himself shall descend from heaven with a shout, with the voice of the archangel, and with the trump of God: and the dead in Christ shall rise first: then we which are alive and remain shall be caught up together with them in the clouds, to meet the Lord in the air: and so shall we ever be with the Lord" (I Thess. 4:16, 17).

The second proof will be the rubble and the ruins of great magnitude, which will result from the sudden disappearance of millions of people from the Earth. Traffic and communication also will be in great turmoil.

The third proof is that a strong military leader will come into power in Western Europe and will establish a ten-nation military rule or coalition.

The fourth proof will be that this military leader (the Antichrist) will make an agreement to guarantee Israel's security in fulfillment of Dan. 9:27.

If these things already have happened by the time you read this book, you will know that you are living in the Tribulation period. That end-time era will last for approximately seven years. It will be a period of severe trials and tribulations as God pours out judgments on the world because of the sins of the people of Earth and for the rejection of His Son, Jesus Christ.

Many people will die during the Tribulation period, but many will manage to live. I write this book so *you* can live, if you are among THOSE WHO REMAIN.

Footnotes

[1] Ezek. 38:3-9; Rev. 17:12, 13; Isaiah 18 and 19.

[2] *World War III and the Destiny of America* has 773 Bible references carefully cross-referenced and indexed. These are compared with more than 100 documented news items that show those prophecies are being fulfilled in this generation. They *all* will see complete fulfillment in this decade! See back of this book for additional information concerning *World War III and the Destiny of America*.

[3]For much more documentation concerning Juan Carlos and Opus
Dei, get the book *Get All Excited — Jesus Is Coming Soon*. It has
16 pages of information about Juan Carlos. See back of this book
for details.

[4]Rev. 8:1-12

FOR 200 YEARS,
NOBODY HAS.

In 1775, eight ships flying this flag prepared to defend our colonies. In the 200 years since, the Navy has never stopped working to keep foreign nations from treading on democracy.

CHAPTER 4

THE DESTINY OF AMERICA

Many are wondering whether America will survive World War III. They are asking, "What is the destiny of America?"

The United States of America has been a nation for only 200 years. It was unknown to Biblical writers. But it *is* in the Bible — by description. And it does fit into the prophecies concerning Israel and World War III.

The U.S.A. is characterized by two terminologies in the Bible.

Description Number One

A complete description of the United States of America is given in Isaiah 18.

It is called *"the land shadowing with wings"* in Isa. 18:1, which easily alludes to our national emblem — the eagle with its outstretched wings.

In verse 2, "the land" being described is narrowed down to *"a nation scattered and peeled"* (KJV) or, more correctly, *"a nation outspread and polished."*

The message is to *a nation* rather than to a continent or a combination of nations. And no other nation in the world is so outspread and highly developed as the U.S.A. Our influence reaches around the world and the people of the United States enjoy the highest standard of living of any nation or people on Earth.

Isa. 18:2 describes the nation of the message as being

"a people terrible from their beginning hitherto."

The Preamble to the Constitution of the United States of America begins: "We, *the people* of the United States, in order to form a more perfect *union* . . ." And this union has formed a nation that has never been defeated in any war since its origin. We are a people to be reckoned with, a people, indeed, "terrible from their beginning . . ." and a nation that the world recognizes as a super-power.

Giving further description, Isa. 18:2 says this nation of the message is "*measured out and trodden down.*" No other nation is so completely surveyed and measured. Every acre is accounted for in the government archives. World Almanac says the United States of America consists of 3,071 counties and 59 county equivalents for a total of 3,130, having a 50-state land area of 3,615,211 square miles traversed by 3,679,-950 lineal miles of roadways and 210,573 miles of railways as of 1966. It most certainly is "*a nation measured out and trodden down.*"

Isa. 18:2 concludes with the declaration, "*whose land the rivers have traversed (cut through).*" According to the Interstate Commerce Commission, the ton mileage carried on U.S. inland waterways in 1976 was 358 billion tons, and this does not include export shipping. With the opening of the Arkansas River Basin Waterway in 1970, wheat and other cargo from the Great Plains now can travel on river barges from within one mile of Tulsa, Oklahoma, direct to the ocean ports and thence to any seaport in the world. Yes, this nation *is* "a nation . . . whose land the rivers have traversed."

Not Ethiopia

Such descriptions as these could not possibly apply to the country of Ethiopia, which is one of the most backward nations in the world. Some Bible expositors have mistakenly applied the message of Isaiah 18 to Ethiopia simply because that name appears in the text. But the message very clearly is to a large, highly developed and powerful nation that is "*beyond* the rivers of Ethiopia." No phase of the description fits Ethiopia.

A Nation of Strength

Isa. 18:3 reads:

> "All ye inhabitants of the world, and dwellers on the
> Earth, see, when he (Uncle Sam, so to speak) lifts up an
> ensign on the mountains . . ."

The U.S.A. has placed its Stars and Stripes on the moon! No other nation has the technology to accomplish this feat and to bring its men back again. And all the world saw this accomplishment by means of our highly technical satellite communications network.

"And when he blows a trumpet, hear" (Isa. 18:3).

When Uncle Sam speaks, whether by the voice of the President or of an ambassador to the United Nations, the whole world hears. Our voice still is a strong one. The United States still is *"a nation terrible from its beginning . . . outspread and polished."*

God's Message to the U.S.A.

The message of Isaiah is one of warning. The first words are

"*Woe* to the land shadowing with wings."

Verse 4 picks up the lament. In it Isaiah declares that the Lord spoke unto him saying,

"I will take my rest, and I will consider in my dwelling place like a clear heat upon herbs, and like a cloud of dew in the heat of harvest" (Isa. 18:4).

The message is that the Lord is going to sit down and consider the actions of this nation. His determinations are not favorable, but are likened to a clear heat upon herbs, which is as detrimental as setting African violets in the bright sunshine. The other comparison is likewise detrimental . . . "like a cloud of dew in the heat of harvest." A heavy cloud of dew at harvest time threatens mildew and crop failure.

America is due for a trimming. Its decadence and sinfulness has come before God and a time of judgment lies ahead.

In poetic form, the warning comes:

"For before the harvest, when the bud is perfect, and the sour grape is ripening in the flower, he shall cut off the sprigs with pruning hooks, and take away and cut down the branches" (Isa. 18:5).

In one verse God says, "*I* will consider . . ." but in the next, God states that a person, identified only as "*he*," shall "cut off" and "cut down" the sprigs and branches of this great nation. The pruning is to happen when this nation is in the prime of its strength, for it is depicted as occurring "when the sour grape is ripening."

Yes, someone is going to greatly cut and damage this nation. But also there is the promise of deliverance. Isa. 18:6 says,

"They shall be left together . . ."

The final message is that this nation will survive its punishment of cutting and pruning and that it will continue as a nation, and the chapter ends with a blessing and a promise:

"In that time shall the present be brought unto the Lord of hosts by a people scattered and peeled, and from a people terrible from their beginning hitherto, a nation measured out and trodden down, whose land the rivers have spoiled (traversed), to the place of the name of the Lord of hosts, the Mount Zion" (Isa. 18:7).

After the Tribulation is over, the United States of America will continue as a nation during the millenial reign of the Lord Jesus Christ, who will rule as Prince of Peace and as KING OF KINGS AND LORD OF LORDS (Rev. 19:11-16). America will bring its present to Him!

Description Number Two

The *pruning* of this country is referred to again in Ezek. 39:6, which says God will send (via Russia) "a fire . . . among them that dwell *carelessly* in the coastlands."

This "careless" nation is alluded to also in Ezek. 30:8, 9:

"And they shall know that I am the Lord, when I have set a fire in Egypt, and when all her helpers shall be destroyed (the Soviet and Warsaw Pact nations, according to Ezekiel 38 and 39). In that day shall messengers be sent forth from me in ships (Soviet nuclear ships?) to make the *careless* Ethiopians afraid, and great pain shall come upon them, as in the days of Egypt: for, lo, it cometh."

The "messengers" of Ezek. 30:9 are the same as the "swift messengers" of Isa. 18:2 sent against the "careless" Americans. By them, America will be severely "cut."

George Washington's Vision

It was 1777, and the winter was severe. Gen. George Washington was at Valley Forge, and he was given a vision in which he saw the future of the United States of America.

He saw the Revolutionary War and its results; the Civil War and its results — even the time when it would occur; and he saw World War III and its climactic results.

The full vision and many proofs of its detailed fulfillments to date are documented in *World War III and the Destiny of America*. The following is a portion of that vision:

End of the Civil War

"As I continued looking, I saw a bright angel on whose brow rested a crown of light on which was traced the word 'UNION.' He was bearing the American flag. He placed the flag between the divided nation and said, 'REMEMBER, YE ARE BRETHREN.'

"The Republic" Develops As "A Nation"

"Instantly, the inhabitants, casting down their weapons, became friends once more and united around the National Standard.

Frightful — Incredible — World War III

"Again I heard the mysterious voice saying, 'SON OF THE REPUBLIC, LOOK AND LEARN.' At this the dark, shadowing angel placed a trumpet to his mouth, and blew three distinct blasts; and taking water from the ocean, he sprinkled it upon Europe, Asia and Africa.

"Then my eyes beheld a fearful scene. From each of these continents arose thick black clouds that were soon joined into one. And through this mass there gleamed a dark RED light by which I saw hordes of armed men. These men, moving with the cloud, marched by land and sailed by sea to America, which country was enveloped in the volume of the cloud. And I dimly saw these armies devastate the whole country and BURN the villages, towns and cities which I had seen springing up.

"As my ears listened to the thundering of the cannon, clashing of swords, and the shouts and cries of MILLIONS IN MORTAL COMBAT, I again heard the mysterious voice saying 'SON OF THE REPUBLIC, LOOK AND LEARN.' When this voice had ceased, the dark, shadowy angel placed his trumpet once more to his mouth, and blew a long and fearful blast.

Heaven Helps the U.S.A.

"Instantly a light as of a thousand suns shone down from above me, and pierced and broke into fragments the dark cloud which enveloped America. At the same moment the angel upon whose head still shown the word 'UNION,' and who bore our national flag in one hand and a sword in the other, descended from the heavens attended by legions of white spirits. These immediately joined the inhabitants of America, who I perceived were well-nigh overcome, but who immediately taking courage again, closed up their broken ranks and renewed the battle.

"Again, amid the fearful noise of the conflict I heard the mysterious voice saying, 'SON OF THE REPUBLIC, LOOK AND LEARN.' As the voice ceased, the shadowy angel for the last time dipped water from the ocean and sprinkled it upon America. INSTANTLY the dark cloud rolled back, together with the armies it had brought, leaving the inhabitants of the land victorious.

The DESTINY of the United States Revealed

"Then once more, I beheld the villages, towns and cities springing up where I had seen them before, while the bright angel, planting the azure standard he had brought in the midst of them, cried with a loud voice: 'WHILE THE STARS REMAIN, AND THE HEAVENS SEND DOWN DEW UPON THE EARTH, SO LONG SHALL THE UNION

LAST.' And taking from his brow the crown on which still blazened the word 'UNION,' he placed it upon the standard while the people kneeling down said, 'AMEN.'

"The scene instantly began to fade and dissolve, and I at last saw nothing but the rising, curling vapor I at first beheld. This also disappeared, and I found myself once more gazing upon the mysterious visitor, who, in the same voice I had heard before, said, 'SON OF THE REPUBLIC, WHAT YOU HAVE SEEN IS THUS INTERPRETED ... THREE GREAT PERILS WILL COME UPON THE REPUBLIC. THE MOST FEARFUL FOR HER IS THE THIRD. BUT THE WHOLE WORLD UNITED SHALL NOT PREVAIL AGAINST HER. LET EVERY CHILD OF THE REPUBLIC LEARN TO LIVE FOR HIS GOD HIS LAND AND UNION.'

"With these words the vision vanished, and I started from my seat and felt that I had seen a vision wherein had been shown me the birth, the progress, and DESTINY of the United States."

Potentials for Fulfillment

Not until this generation has there been the scientific development and massive military build-up sufficient to fulfill the latter part of the vision. But it can happen today!

Russia has a huge missile capacity. Since the Cuban missile crisis in 1962, Russia has become a great superpower with a fearful spectre of 2,378 strategic missiles with an explosive power of 10,000 megatons (10 billion *tons* of TNT).[1]

This is more than twice the megatonage in the United States arsenal.

Russia has 73 missile submarines to our 41 and 253 attack submarines to our 73. We lead in tactical aircraft, but Russia leads in major combat ships. In tanks, the United States has 10,000 against Russia's 42,000. And in armed forces our 2,084,-350 service personnel would face a formidable Soviet army of 4,412,000.[2]

"The Russians are going for superiority," says a senior U.S. general. "They want to dominate, to get war-winning capability."[3]

Russia has mighty forces today, and the U.S. is increasing

constantly. But we can no longer be passive. When the war comes — and it will because it is prophesied in the Bible — the destruction will be tremendous.

Further evidence of the danger of the buildup is seen in the following:

> *Jan. 26, 1979*, Los Angeles Times: "WASHINGTON — Defense Secretary Harold Brown said Thursday that the Soviet Union is building its nuclear missile force at a faster pace than was anticipated a year ago, increasing the danger that the 1980s may become an era of Soviet strategic superiority . . . He cited the growth in the Russian military as 'potentially very dangerous to us.' "

> *June 16, 1979*, The Register, Orange Co.: "WASHINGTON (AP) — Gen. Bernard Rogers, the Army's chief of staff, predicted Friday that the United States will be strategically weaker than Russia in the early 1980s and expressed concern that Russia may then test this country's resolve.

> " 'We are losing essential equivalence on the strategic side,' Rogers told a group of reporters."

> *Oct. 14, 1979*, Los Angeles Times: "WASHINGTON- (UPI) — Led by the Soviet Union and the United States, the world is spending a record $434 billion a year on military might, the U.S. Arms Control and Disarmament Agency said Saturday.

> "The Soviet Union and the United States in 1977 accounted for more than half the world's military spending — $140 billion by the Soviets and $101 billion by the United States."

The Soviets are gaining superiority because they are spending many billions of dollars more on armaments — far more than needed for defense purposes. The intent is obvious. It is no longer a matter of question as to whether there will be a World War III: it is only a matter of *how soon*?

THOSE WHO REMAIN after the conflict will exist in a post-nuclear environment of devastation and famine. The Bible predicts that it will take a full day's wages to buy one loaf of bread. And it says one-fourth of mankind will die as a result of the war and the famine that follows (Rev. 6:6-8).

Christians can be very thankful that coordinated Bible

prophecy definitely shows the *rapture of the Church* will take place *before* World War III. And as we see the great potential for that war today, we cannot help but look up, for our "redemption draweth nigh" (Luke 21:28). JESUS IS COMING SOON!

As I consider these things, however, my great concern is for THOSE WHO REMAIN and how they will survive.

Footnotes

[1] Statistics accurate as of March 1, 1976.
[2] U.S. Library of Congress report, *Newsweek*, Mar. 1, 1976.
[3] *NEWSWEEK*, Mar. 1, 1976.

POWER ON PARADE. Massive buildup of conventional military strength has led to "greater Russian adventurism in places far beyond Soviet borders."

U.S. News & World Report, Oct. 30, 1978

I am come that they might have Life.   (John 10:10)

CHAPTER 5

SURVIVAL

Before we examine more closely events that will come, there is a matter of greater importance to consider.

How can you be sure of living through the holocaust of World War III? And what will happen to you if you don't?

God has an answer.

It won't make any difference how good or how bad you lived. The Bible says, "*All* have sinned and come short of the glory of God" (Rom. 3:23).

You and I are human, and we have failed to live perfect lives. This means we need a Saviour. We need someone to redeem us from the wages of sin, which is death (Rom. 6:23).

Years ago, someone told me about Jesus and His great love. And when I trusted in His sacrifice of His own life for me, He took my sins upon Himself and gave to me His Life.

He can do the same for you. He can give you eternal Life — if you only ask Him for it.

Salvation is a gift of and from God, but we must ask Him for it. And we must take God's Word that He will give it to us.

Jesus said, "Come unto me, all of you who are weak and are heavy laden with sin." He said, "*Whosoever* cometh to me, I will not cast away." God's Word says, "Believe on the Lord Jesus Christ and you *shall* be saved" (Matt. 11:28; John 6:37; Acts 16:31).

What are we to believe?

Believe that when Christ died on the cruel cross of Calvary, He died for the sins of all who would call upon Him. This includes me. It includes *you*. Yes, you are the "whosoever" that He wants to save today. Will you take Him at His word? Will you trust Him?

Jesus loves you. That's the very reason He laid this message upon my heart for you. He wants to save your spirit and soul so you can live with Him and with all the family of

God in absolute peace and harmony for all eternity. He can give you a new spirit — right now.

Nothing in this world is as important as your soul. There is a hell, but God doesn't want you to go there.

He gave His own Son, the Lord Jesus Christ, as a sacrifice for you. Jesus suffered and bled and died for you. What you and I could not do, He did for us. God honored Jesus for His obedience and raised Him from the dead.

We don't come to a dead Jesus; He is the living Lord Jesus Christ. After He arose from the dead, He told His disciples, "Go into all the world and preach the Gospel." Christ was then taken up into Heaven to live with God the Father *until* everyone hears the Gospel who will listen.

This message is God's invitation to you to believe in His Son and to trust in Him for your own salvation.

Will you bow your head and say a short prayer with me right now? It is your gateway to eternal life. You can repeat these words:

> **"Dear God in Heaven, I do believe that Jesus loves me and wants to save me. I know that I have done wrong. I know that I am a sinner. Please forgive me for my sins. I do believe that Jesus gave His life to save sinners. Please save me now! I ask this in the name of Jesus who died for me. I believe that He loved me, and I give Him my sins and my life right now. I accept Jesus Christ as my personal Saviour. THANK YOU, Lord, for hearing my prayer. I rejoice in my new life. THANK YOU, JESUS, for saving me. I thank you and I praise you as my Lord. Amen!"**

Jesus has promised in His Word never to leave you nor forsake you. As you said this prayer with a sincere heart, He became your Saviour for all of eternity. With your salvation, God has given you an obligation and a responsibility to tell others about the love of Jesus and about His wonderful salvation. You will find great joy in telling others about your salvation, and the only greater joy is to see the one to whom you are witnessing accept Jesus Christ as his or her personal Saviour.

I sincerely hope and trust you have the opportunity to read this book and accept Jesus Christ as your Saviour before *the rapture of the church.* If you did, you will be taken up into heaven with the rest of the believers in Christ when He comes. And that will be very soon!

In the event you did *not* accept Jesus Christ as your Saviour before the true Christians were taken into heaven, read on. I will instruct you as best I can.

First, say the prayer quoted in this chapter; believe it, and trust in Jesus Christ right now.

As an evidence of your salvation and as a witness of your sincerity, sign one of the lines provided below. That act will be your personal confession of Jesus Christ as your own Saviour, your Redeemer.

_____

_____

_____

_____

Now read on, for great events and dangers lie ahead!

French H-bomb exploding over South Pacific atoll in 1971: The nuclear race goes on

Black Star

Poseidon (MIRV) missile launched from the nuclear powered fleet ballistic missile submarine USS Daniel Boone.

CHAPTER 6

FUTURE EVENTS

As I write this book, the next great event to take place is the *rapture of the Church.* THOSE WHO REMAIN will face the terrible holocaust of World War III and the *Tribulation period.*

As we've already seen, a man will rise to great political and military power in Europe in the wake of the chaos caused by the disappearance of millions of people around the globe.

He will seem to have all the answers to the world's problems and will claim to have the ability to guarantee Israel's protection against attack from Russia and the Arabs.

He will assume the military leadership of the European Community on the condition that he be allowed to replace three of the original ten nations of the Common Market with three nations of his own choosing.[1] News events as of this writing strongly indicate that the next three into the Common Market could well be Spain, Portugal and Austria, for these nations already have applied for membership and Spain is way ahead of the others in negotiation and preparation. And Spain does have the strongest military king Europe has seen since Charlemagne was crowned Emperor of the West in A.D. 800. Watch Juan Carlos.

Whoever the Antichrist turns out to be, he will enter into the World War III confrontation with the Arabs and Soviets when they strike in force against Israel. From this war, he will emerge as the victor and by conquest will be in full control of all of the old Roman Empire region. Then, with "great fury"[2] he will conquer much territory, becoming a world ruler of great esteem. He is to be a man of war and *not* of peace as some teachers seem to think. His guarantee of peace is only with Israel.

Jerusalem

Now, let's take a closer look at the Antichrist's intentions for Jerusalem. In Dan. 9:26, it is written:

> "And the people of the prince that shall come shall des-
> troy the city and the sanctuary."

The Romans destroyed Jerusalem and tore down the
Hebrew temple in A.D. 70. It has never been rebuilt. The time
for that restoration is just ahead of us. And the man who will
make the covenant with Israel and allow the Jews to rebuild
the temple in Jerusalem will be the Antichrist king.

Daniel continues his prophecy in verse 27:

> "In the *midst* of the week (of years — after 3½ years),
> he will cause the sacrifice and the offerings to cease."

The Orthodox Jews will have their temple and conduct
animal sacrifices and altar worship in Jerusalem during the
first half of the Tribulation period. Their temple worship
ceases, however, at the middle of Daniel's prophetic week.

That the Antichrist king will be in authority during the en-
tire seven-year Tribulation period is verified by Rev. 11:2 and
Rev. 13:5.

> "But the court which is outside the temple, leave out,
> and measure it not; for it is given unto the Gentiles; and
> the holy city shall they tread under foot forty-two
> months."

> "And there was given unto him a mouth speaking
> great things and blasphemies; and power was given unto
> him to *continue* forty-two months."

Antichrist will break the covenant "in the midst of the
week" and will "continue" forty-two months (another 3½
years) speaking "great things and blasphemies."

When Satan is cast out of the heavens (Rev. 12:9) and
enters the physical body of the Antichrist at the middle of the
Tribulation, *he will* speak great things. *Then* will come the act
of abomination spoken of by Daniel and by Jesus and prophesied in II Thess. 2:4,

> "So that he as God sitteth in the temple of God, shew-
> ing himself that he is God."

In blasphemy, he will demand worship. It is during the *last
half* of the Tribulation period, therefore, that all people will be

compelled to bow down to him and receive "the mark of the beast" in their forehead or their right hand.

Do not forget the warning given at the end of chapter 2 of this book. Any who receive "the mark of the beast" will be branded with Satan as one of his worshippers and will be doomed for all eternity, going to be with Satan in the lake of fire that burns forever and ever, The Devil is a loser. Jesus Christ as KING OF KINGS AND LORD OF LORDS[6] will defeat and destroy the Antichrist at the end of the seven-year Tribulation period.

God's Two Prophets

Simultaneously with the revealing of Antichrist in Western Europe, two other men will gain world prominence. Their ministry will be in Jerusalem. As mighty prophets of God, the Bible says they will have power to control the elements.

They will bring drought, and they will be able to turn water into blood. They will strike the world with many plagues — all this during the first half of the Tribulation.

Because of their great harmful powers, many people will try to kill them. But they won't succeed. And those who try will be killed themselves because the two prophets will have power to call down fire from Heaven to destroy their enemies (Rev. 11:5).

When the Antichrist leader becomes indwelt by Satan, *he* will succeed in killing the prophets. Their dead bodies will lie in the streets of Jerusalem for three-and-a-half days. The Bible says the people will rejoice over them and will "make merry, and shall send gifts one to another because these two prophets tormented them that dwelt on the earth."

But their rejoicing will be cut short. After three-and-a-half days, the spirit of life from God will enter into their bodies, and they will stand to their feet. Then a great voice from Heaven will call them saying, "Come up here." And they will be seen to ascend from Earth to Heaven. Rev. 11:9 says *all* the nations will witness this phenomenon.

(The World's satellite communications systems now in operation make this the first generation that could possibly see the fulfillment of such an amazing prophecy.)

God's 144,000 Witnesses

Still another drama will unfold over the Earth, this also during the first half of the Tribulation.

At the very beginning of the Tribulation, an angel will place a special mark, the name of the Father, on the forehead of 144,000 Jewish men (Rev. 7:2-8; 14:1). They will become God's special witnesses to mankind. The 144,000 is comprised of 12,000 men from each of twelve tribes of Israel. These Jewish messengers will preach the Gospel of the Kingdom (Matt. 24:14) to all the world. In that kingdom-to-come, the returned Christ will rule from Jerusalem, the city of David.

Don't be deceived by those who proclaim a kingdom gospel today — before the events of the Tribulation begin. They don't have God's identifying mark on their foreheads, and their message is false. They don't honor Christ *as the Son of God*.

The Bible says, "Believe on the Lord Jesus Christ and thou shalt be saved" (Acts 16:31). This is the message that you must believe; there is no other way of salvation.

With all evangelical church leaders and ministers gone (in the rapture), the message will be that Christ is soon to return as King of the Jews and as KING OF KINGS AND LORD OF LORDS.

If you are here at that time, listen to these men, for their message will be the way of salvation during the first half of the Tribulation period.

The ministry of the 144,000 Jewish witnesses will be *only* during the first half of the seven-year Tribulation period. They will be killed by the Antichrist when their ministry is completed. But he can't harm them during their time of service because of God's seal upon them.

When Satan is cast out of the heavens onto Earth (Rev. 12:9), he then will be able to kill them — just as he will kill the two prophets who minister with them during the first 3½ years.

Those who have believed the Gospel of the Kingdom also will be slain at the middle of the Tribulation. This is prophesied in Rev. 13:7 —

"And it was given unto him to make war with the saints, and to overcome them; and power was given him over all kindreds, and tongues, and nations."

If you are living at that time, don't be afraid of the death that will come by the hand of Antichrist. A martyr's crown will be yours in Heaven. (Rev. 2:10).

Those who die for their faith in Jesus will be given robes of righteousness in Heaven; they also will be privileged to be before God's throne to serve Him.

It is far better to die as a Christian martyr than to follow the end-time false church system and Antichrist into eternal destruction.

The False Church

At the beginning of the seven-year Tribulation period, a false world church system will come into being.

The ecumenical church systems will unite into a worldwide apostate organization, with its international headquarters in Rome (Rev. 17:9, 18).

It will not proclaim the Gospel as we know it, but will advocate free love and permit all sorts of abominations. In Rev. 17:5, this apostate church is called *Babylon the great, the mother of harlots and abominations of the Earth.*

Those who heed the Gospel of the Kingdom will be persecuted by the false church; they will be hunted down and slain (Rev. 6:9-11; 17:6; 13:7). And the power of that social welfare organization will be so strong that it will force people to worship only in its churches.

The Bible implies that evangelical churches will be eliminated. The false church will stamp out all evangelical works and seek to destroy all saving faith in Jesus Christ as Redeemer. Rev. 17:6 declares:

"And I saw the woman (symbol of the false church) drunken with the blood of the saints, and with the blood of the martyrs of Jesus."

The "church" of the Tribulation will be full of lust and sinfulness, allowing free love and many abominable acts. It will be a conglomerate of many churches of many religious systems, which will set itself up as *the* church. It will originate in Rome, but will soon move to Babylon[13] (Zech. 5:5-11; Rev. 18).

The Antichrist king will tolerate this wicked form of church system and let it prosper because it poses no threat to him. But in the middle of the Tribulation, when Satan is cast out of the heavenlies and enters into the body of Antichrist, he will demand that all people worship *him* and him only. Babylon, future headquarters of the world church, will be destroyed by fire at that time — most likely by atomic fire, for the Bible indicates that the destruction of the city of Babylon will be "in one hour" (Rev. 18:19; Isa. 13:19-22). It will never be rebuilt after that final destruction by fire (Isa. 13:20).

What You Can Do

Physical survival and protection will be greatly important at this time. But even more important will be the spiritual decisions you will face.

The first thing you can do is pray.

Terrible times are about to come upon this polluted world. Not only has man polluted God's creation with debris and all kinds of contaminates, he has polluted his own soul with lust, greed and self-indulgence.

This sin must be purged and cleansed.

But God will not leave you without hope or means of escape. However, at this time — during the Tribulation — the price of deliverance will be very heavy.

You can still be saved because God has promised you the opportunity to decide. If you are reading this, and the Tribulation has already begun, you can still decide for Christ. You will not immediately join your loved ones who have gone to Heaven; but you can still attain salvation and join them in the near future.

Before this can happen, however, you need to ask God to forgive you for all of your sins and trust in Jesus who died on the cross to pay the penalty for your sins.

Jesus Christ so loved you that He gave His life as a ransom for your soul. But YOU must make the final arrangement. You can choose to accept His ransom, or reject it. Jesus is waiting for your decision. The Bible says, "Believe on the

Lord Jesus Christ and thou shalt be saved" (Acts 16:31).

If you will accept this simple message of salvation, bow your head right now — wherever you are — and repeat this prayer to God:

"Dear God in Heaven, I admit that I am a sinner. I am truly sorry for my sins. Please forgive me and save me, for I ask it in the name of Jesus who died for me. I trust in Jesus right now, and I believe that His perfect blood cleanses me from all of my sin. It is all-sufficient for me. I thank you for hearing my prayer, and I thank you for saving my soul. I am now a child of God by faith in Jesus Christ. I thank you in the name of Jesus. Amen."

God inspired the Scripture which says, "WHOSOEVER SHALL CALL UPON THE NAME OF THE LORD SHALL BE SAVED." That "whosoever" includes everyone. It includes you. And it includes me. His divine Word still stands. If your confession was genuine and from your heart, verify it by signing your name on the line below:

_____

If you were fortunate enough to read this book and to receive Jesus Christ as your Saviour *before* the return of Christ for His believing Body, the Church, you will be taken into Heaven with us when that great moment arrives.

If You Delay

But if you read this book and don't accept Christ before the split second when Christ comes for His own, you will be left behind. The choice is up to you.

If, however, you did not receive this book and did not have a chance to trust in Christ as your Saviour before His return, you can still be saved. Say "the sinner's prayer" quoted above, put your faith and trust in Jesus as Saviour and Lord, and sign your name as a testimony of your faith.

Your life now will be in grave danger. The anti-God and Antichrist king of this world has just become your mortal enemy. He will kill you or cause you to be killed if any one of his host of informers can get to you.

Let me extend this additional warning to you. If you read this message, and for fear of your very short earthly life you do *not* accept Jesus Christ as your personal Saviour and Redeemer; and if, in order to save your neck, you submit to the wiles of the deceiver and ever bow down to him, you will face a far greater loss.

You will be doomed and damned for all eternity and will be banished forever from any part of Heaven.

It is either accept a loving and a merciful Jesus as Saviour, or follow after and accept the condemnation of a Satan-indwelt deceiver called the Antichrist. The choice is up to you.

In the course of the events of this world there must come a time of reckoning. That time has arrived.

Footnotes

1 Dan. 7:8, 24; 11:39

2 Dan. 11:44

3 Rev. 13:5

4 Rev. 12:7-9

5 Rev. 13:3-5

6 Rev. 19:11-20

7 Rev. 11:10

8 Rev. 7:2-8; 4:1

9 Rev. 7:2-3

10 Rev. 2:10

11 Rev. 17:3-9, 18

12 Rev. 6:9-11; 17:6; 13:7

13 Zech. 5:5-11; Rev. 18. The ancient city of Babylon is being rebuilt in Iraq today. Even the tower of Babel is being reconstructed as a tourist attraction. *Hillah* is within the boundaries of ancient Babylon and has a present population of over 85,000. As reported in The Los Angeles Times, Dec. 3, 1975, UCLA and the University of Turin, Italy, are working with the Iraqi Department of antiquities in this reconstruction. (Update) — *Jan. 28, 1980, The Miami Herald:* "A team from Kyoto University is working to restore Babylon in part and to reconstruct the famous Tower of Babel ... The Iraqi government wants to make Babylon a 'museum city,' a Disneyland, Middle East. Why the Japanese? The Iraqis won't deal with the West because it liberated many architectural treasures now in Western museums. And Japan imports $35 billion worth of oil a year from the Arab countries."

14 Isa. 13:20

15 Rom. 10:13

CHAPTER 7

LIFE AFTER THE BOMB

Destruction potential is so great in this nuclear age that nobody wants to think about it, and few people talk about it.

But the U.S. Government has spent many millions of dollars for research on survival in America after World War III.

The following is taken from a special article by Roger Rapoport (author of the NORAD report) as it appeared in WEST magazine October 10, 1971:

"The seers of California's think tanks, in concert with their fellow analysts around the nation, have probed deeper into the ultimate human crisis and come up with a lot of food for thought.

"The peril is nuclear war and their mission is to map the road to recovery after the fall-out clears. Over the past decade the Pentagon's Office of Civil Defense (OCD) and the Atomic Energy Commission have spent over $86 million to figure out how the public can live better radio-actively. A healthy portion of this research budget has gone to groups like the Rand Corporation in Santa Monica and the Stanford Research Institute up north in Menlo Park . . .

"Most Americans do not look forward to life after nuclear war. But the OCD says that is because they do not realize post-attack society will offer certain advantages over pre-attack society. Rent, taxes and consumer debts may all be canceled. Abandonment of old people, chronic invalids and the insane will lighten the welfare load. Per capita wealth will increase, and it seems likely that everyone will get a promotion. No one will starve because there will be plenty of potato chips to go around.

"So the enemy penetrates our defense system — that does not mean the world has come to an end. Do not panic about being packed into a community fallout shelter. Actually the overcrowding 'is effective in reducing fatalities to occupants,' provided 'overheating is not a serious problem.' Just be sure to bring along your sleeping pills and Bible, says the OCD. Before you know it, you will be ready for evacuation to the country.

"For example, Los Angeles residents can look forward to relocation in the desert — a delightful change of pace, as long as you remember to bring along your air conditioner. Others will be moved to mountain caverns, a good place to be as long as you bring along your down parka . . .

"Even in the worst attacks the experts remain optimistic about survival prospects: 'I can write you any kind of nuclear war scenario you want,' says Dr. H. H. Mitchell of the Rand Corporation. 'But no matter how bad the war is, man is going to survive. Even if a billion people are killed you still have a couple billion left' . . . Dr. Mitchell and the other post-attack researchers for OCD and AEC stay sane by writing reports that make Armageddon sound palatable . . . Likewise, Human Science Research, Incorporated, concludes that the news media should have little trouble operating with a skeleton staff of survivors when the war is over: 'A typical newspaper of 35 pages contains less than three pages of essential news . . . The news media thus should be able to carry out their tasks under . . . emergency conditions because their task can be reduced . . .'

"A 137-page report published by the Stanford Research Institute suggests how Hitler's wartime industrial controls could be useful in post-attack society . . .

"At the Rand Corporation, scientists justify the most preposterous postwar ideas by claiming they are telling 'what is likely to be done rather than what should be done' after the bomb falls. Under this cover, Rand demographer Ira S. Lowry talks about how to rebuild society in an AEC study on the post-attack population of the U.S.:

" 'Depending on the international environment, public priorities might go either to restoring the nation's military strength or to rebuilding the industrial plant. Whichever the goal, the relevant view of the nation's population is as both resource and burden . . . Survivors . . . in their productive years — roughly 15 to 63 by present standards — would clearly be the most valuable segment of the post-attack population. They would have to be kept in good health and encouraged to produce their utmost, to go where they were needed, to transfer their skills from frivolous to serious occupations . . .

" 'Policymakers would presumably have to draw the line somewhere, however, in making such concessions, and those most likely to suffer are people with little or no productive potential: old people, chronic invalids and the insane. Old people suffer the special disadvantage of being easily identified as a group and therefore subject to categorical treatment . . . Since the amount of care and attention necessary to sustain life increases with age, this drain on national resources could significantly affect recovery planning. In this sense, at least, a community under stress would be better off without its old and feeble members.'

"And just how would we go about this? Well, Lowry thinks: 'The easiest way to implement a morally repugnant but socially beneficial policy is by inaction . . . failing to make any special provision for the special needs of the elderly, the insane and the chronically ill . . . overall the share of the elderly in the national product would drop.

" 'Public policy toward surviving children would probably be more generous. The nearer these are to labor-force age, the greater their present value as producers, and the less costly it would be to protect them . . .'

The Fate of Free Enterprise

"The fate of free enterprise is a prime concern of all post-attack research. A broad Stanford Research Institute study looks at post-attack food availability in five American cities: San Jose, Albuquerque, New Orleans, Providence and Detroit. The scientists conduct simulated attacks and then calculate the fate of every food processor in town . . .

"These SRI studies show that survivors will initially experience certain privations in post-attack society. The Albuquerque report says that during the first month after nuclear war 'survivors may anticipate severe shortages of every commodity except potatoes.' Fluid milk will be the scarcest item because of 'depletion of local dairy herds due to radiation sickness' and contamination of the milk produced by surviving cows. The milk will be usable only when put into a processed form, like cheese, and aged so that its radioactivity can decay to safe levels. Although meat, eggs, vegetables and other staples will be available, blast damage should temporarily inhibit their transport to market . . . A severe sugar shortage may also hurt the makers of 'bakery products, sweetened condensed milk, canned fruits, jams and jellies, and confectionary products.'

"But despite these problems, no one will starve. One 'particularly valuable post-attack crop' — the potato — should make it. 'The survival of much of the national harvest, coupled with the immediate availability of the local crop, guarantees that Albuquerque survivors will not lack potatoes at any time during the first post-attack year' . . ."

And so on and on go the endless government research reports. Survival will be possible but difficult in a post-attack society. But the fact remains that the United States government is deeply concerned, for it realizes that a nuclear war is coming, like it or not.

Crisis Relocation Planning

The Pentagon is developing plans to use abandoned mines as nuclear fall-out shelters and to move millions of Americans into them during times of crisis.

"Our estimates now," says a researcher for the Defense Department's Civil Preparedness Agency (DCPA), "are that under Crisis Relocation Planning criteria, there is a potential for sheltering 50 million people in level, dry and readily accessible mines."

The DCPA says it has already found space for "6 million in some 2,000 mines" around the country. Montana, Utah and Missouri are cited as states with lots of usable mine shafts. According to DCPA research, 70 per cent of the population of Missouri would fit into the state's mines and caves.

The plan to put people in mines and caves to protect them from nuclear attack is part of a new Civil Defense program called Crisis Relocation. Under Crisis Relocation, the populations of all major U.S. cities and other "high risk" areas such as military installations would be evacuated to "low risk" areas during periods of "international tension."

DCPA officials acknowledge that even if everything "worked perfectly," 50 to 135 million Americans would still die in an all-out attack. But they say those statistics only emphasize the importance of proper planning.

If the United States government feels this much responsibility and senses this much urgency about the current international situation, how much more should *we Christians* note that the world is coming to crisis? It is not coming to an end, but it *is* coming to crisis, and it is very rapidly moving into the exact end-time alignments that were prophesied so many centuries ago. God caused the ancient prophets to write that which we know as the Bible. Its predictions are true. Let's pay attention to them.

What to Do

Since a battle by fire (World War III) is positively prophesied in the Bible, what should we do?

There are two things that can be done: first, know what the Bible says; second, respond accordingly.

The Bible contains more specific information about events that are to happen in this generation than is told about any other period in all of history. We are now living in *the decade of destiny*.

The *rapture of the Church* will occur in this era.

The wily king called the Antichrist will soon come into power; the thermonuclear exchange called World War III, the advent of two great Hebrew prophets in Jerusalem and the preaching of "the Gospel of the kingdom" by 144,000 *Jewish* messengers that will have the seal of God visibly inscribed in their foreheads, will take place in our generation.

Many great earthquakes will occur, severe plagues will come upon the Earth, and a tremendous struggle for existence will transpire around the world (including the United States of America).

THOSE WHO REMAIN is written that you might have specific information concerning the events that are about to come to pass. Listen to the warnings. They are not fiction.

They are the explanations of Bible prophecy, which is history proclaimed in advance.

How to Survive

The United States government is aware of Russia's intentions. The Pentagon has allocated more than $100 million for research and study projects such as Crisis Relocation and reports of the Office of Civil Defense (OCD) and the Atomic Energy Commission (AEC).

"Safe" areas have been outlined on maps of the Defense Department's Civil Preparedness Agency (DCPA) and plans have been made for mass evacuation from "target" areas to relatively safer ones in the deserts, mines and caves. Follow their directions if you have time.

When *the rapture* takes place, my instruction to THOSE WHO REMAIN is to pray first, asking God for salvation and help.

Then, from a practical standpoint, leave all target areas (cities over 200,000 population; Army, Navy and Air Force centers; strategic industrial areas and seacoast cities). Take food in cans, bottles and sealed containers to guard against radioactivity from atomic fallout resulting from the tremendous thermonuclear war.

Be sure to take drinking water in sealed containers. The Bible warns that "many men will die of the waters, because they were made bitter" (Rev. 8:11). Don't drink from open streams!

Stay away from known earthquake faults because the Bible predicts that many earthquakes will take place. (They are increasing in number already!) If in California, locate *east* of the San Andreas fault line, for a combination of earthquakes and huge tidal waves may wreck the West Coast.

When you get located inland, dig a good fallout shelter. A Geiger counter also will be helpful for testing radioactivity in the air as well as in water and foodstuffs. You may have to "button up" for two or three weeks to let radioactive dust and debris settle.

Don't wait for the war to start. It will come so quickly you

South Bay Daily Breeze, Torrance, Ca. — April 10, 1974

wouldn't have a chance. Where could you go in thirty minutes?

And if you have a gun, take it with you, plus a good supply of ammunition. Marauders, anarchists and opportunists will be armed and dangerous. This will be especially true when food becomes scarce.

Famine is one of the side-effects of the war that will cause one-fourth of mankind to die. This is also specific Bible prophecy.

But three-fourths of mankind will live, and you *will* have a chance to survive. When you do, be thankful. Put your trust in Jesus Christ for your salvation — and for your safety.

Many great things are going to happen. The question is, "How soon?"

Soviet Tanks in Afghanistan.

CHAPTER 8

POSSIBLE TIME
OF THE CLIMAX

Many students of eschatology (the science of last things) believe the coming of Jesus Christ for His Body, the Church, will be on the Feast of Trumpets and as a fulfillment of that God-ordained feast.

The Bible reasons for this teaching are explained in detail in my book *Get All Excited — Jesus Is Coming Soon.*

In brief, here is the reasoning:

The Lord God, Yahvah, The Existing One, set the exact day for each of the holy feasts of the people of Israel. Those feast days are listed in the third book of the Bible. Leviticus 23 begins:

> "And the Lord spoke unto Moses, saying, Speak unto the children of Israel and say to them, Concerning the feasts of the Lord, which ye shall proclaim to be holy convocations, even *these are my feasts.*"

God emphasized the matter again in verse 37 saying,

> "These are the feasts of the Lord, which ye shall proclaim to be holy convocations unto you, to offer an offering . . . *everything upon his day.*"

That chapter closes with the words,

> "And Moses declared unto the children of Israel *the feasts of the Lord*" (Lev. 23:44).

It is important to notice that the Lord God set the exact day for each of the holy convocations (gatherings of the people) and declared that each feast must be *"upon his day."*

Fulfillments of the Feast Days

Jesus fulfilled the Feast of Passover when He died on the cross of Calvary at 3 p.m. Nisan 14, A.D. 30. It was the appointed time of the Passover sacrifice.

Jesus fulfilled the Feast of Unleavened Bread in that His body, broken for us, lay in the tomb on that day (Nisan 15).

Jesus fulfilled the Feast of Firstfruits in that He arose from the dead on that day, the first day of the week following Passover.

Jesus fulfilled the Feast of Weeks (Pentecost) in that on that specific day He sent the Holy Spirit into the world.[1]

The next feast to be fulfilled is Feast of Trumpets. Since Jesus fulfilled each of the others, and did so on the exact day of each, it is logical to expect that He will fulfill the Feast of Trumpets also on its exact day, Tishri 1. Note these passages of Scripture:

> "For the *trumpet* shall sound, and the dead shall be raised incorruptible, and we shall be changed" (I Cor. 15:52).
>
> "For the Lord himself shall descend from heaven with a shout, with the voice of the archangel, and with the *trump* of God: and the dead in Christ shall rise first: then we which are alive and remain shall be caught up together with them in the clouds, to meet the Lord in the air: and so shall we ever be with the Lord" (I Thess. 4:16, 17).

Whatever year our Lord returns, Bible prophecy would most appropriately be fulfilled if His return occurred on Feast of Trumpets.

I am not a prophet. I can't predict. But I *do* have a sense of expectancy because the overwhelming evidence indicates that time is running out.

Jesus said, "When ye shall see all these things, know that it is near, even at the door . . . This generation shall not pass till all these things be fulfilled" (Matt. 24:33, 34).

"This generation," therefore, will witness the fulfillment of *all* prophecies from the rebirth of Israel as a nation to the coming of Christ as Messiah at the end of the Tribulation period. It refers to the era that will see *His* return.

I believe this Biblical generation began in 1948 when Israel was recognized officially as a nation by the U.N. General Assembly.

Hebrew Leap Year?

At one time, I expected the Lord's return would need to be in a Hebrew leap year to allow seven months from the Feast of Trumpets to Passover to provide time for burying the dead slain during World War III (Ezek. 39:12). But another Scripture reference has come to my attention that nullifies that thought. Numbers 9:9-11 says:

> "And the Lord spake unto Moses, saying, Speak unto the children of Israel, saying, If any man of you or of your posterity shall be unclean by reason of a dead body, or be in a journey afar off, yet he shall keep the passover unto the Lord.
>
> "The fourteenth day of the second month at even they shall keep it."

This is God's "contingency clause." If a person cannot observe the Feast of Passover on its regular day because he is defiled by having touched the body of a person that is dead, then that person can observe the Feast of Passover one month later — on the 14th day of the *second* month. Passover was always to be on the 14th day of the first month, Nisan.

Thus it is that even in a regular year the Feast of Passover can be observed by the people of Israel at its appointed time six months after the previous Feast of Trumpets; and the ones personally defiled because they were still burying the dead from the great war of Ezekiel 38 and 39 can keep the feast one month later, after they have completed burying the dead. The return of the Lord at the time of the rapture, therefore, is not restricted just to a Hebrew leap year. It could be at any time in any year within "this generation," but most likely on the day of the Feast of Trumpets in whichever year He comes for His own. BE READY.

Footnotes

[1] Refer to John 15:26; Acts 2:1-4.

Time for the Third Temple?

Some Jews see plausible theological grounds for discussing reconstruction of the Temple. They base their argument on the contention that Israel has already entered its "Messianic era."

In 1948, they note, Israel's chief rabbis ruled that with the establishment of the Jewish state and the "ingathering of the exiles," the age of redemption had begun. Today, many of Israel's religious leaders are convinced that the Jewish victories over the Arabs has taken Judaism well beyond that point.

Says Historian Israel Eldad: "We are at the stage where David was when he liberated Jerusalem. From that time until the construction of the Temple by Solomon, only one generation passed. So will it be with us." And what about that Moslem shrine? Answers Eldad: "It is of course an open question. Who knows? Perhaps there will be an earthquake."

CHAPTER 9

THIS GENERATION

The disciples were anxious for the Lord to set up His kingdom on Earth. They asked Him, "When shall these things be?"

In reply, Jesus gave them many signs as recorded in Matthew 24, Mark 13 and Luke 21. Then He said,

> **"Now learn a parable of the fig tree: When his branch is yet tender and putteth forth leaves, ye know that summer is nigh: So likewise ye, when ye shall see all these things, know that it is near, even at the doors. Verily I say unto you, This generation shall not pass, till *all* these things be fulfilled" (Matt. 24:32-34).**

Israel is recognized as being the nation of the fig tree. Virtually all Bible scholars agree that when it revived as a nation May 14, 1948, *that was the beginning* of what Jesus referred to as "this generation." Before it passes, all prophecy pertaining to the Second Coming will be fulfilled up to and including "the anointing of the most Holy,"[1] which refers to His consecration and presentation as the Messiah, the Deliverer of Israel. This occurs at the end of the seven-year Tribulation period.

70 Years?

Bible prophecy reveals that 70 weeks of years are involved in the prophecies concerning the Messiah: 69 weeks of years (Dan. 9:25) plus one (70th) week of seven years (Dan. 9:27). The 69 weeks were completed when Jesus, the suffering Messiah of Isa. 53, was "cut off, but not for himself."[2]

The final covenant week of years is future and will see its fulfillment as soon as the Antichrist king of the end time comes into power, making his seven-year covenant to guarantee Israel's security for that period of time. *Today*, Israel is seeking just such a guarantee. The time is near at hand!

Since "70" is so significant in Jewish prophecy, there is a theory that 70 years after the Balfour Declaration, Israel will have its sovereignty and peace. Messiah will come.

If this holds true, and Jesus comes as Messiah the King in 1987 (1917 + 70 = 1987): on that basis, His return for His Body, the Church, would be seven years prior — in 1980. This is possible.

40-Year Generation

Two segments of time have been suggested for the length of a Bible generation: 35 years and 40 years.

It is stated in Job 42:16 that Job lived 140 years after his trials, "even four generations." Since 140 divided by 4 equals 35, one logical conclusion is that one generation *could be* 35 years.

I was among many who proclaimed this possibility in case it held to be true. Time would clarify it one way or another. Now it is evident that more than 35 years has to be involved, because 35 years from 1948 would be 1983. If that were the time for Messiah to come in power, then the Tribulation would have begun seven years earlier — in 1976. But the rapture did not occur then, and neither was the Antichrist revealed who could sign a seven-year treaty with Israel. As of this writing, those events are still in the future.

Today, nearly all Bible prophecy scholars consider a Bible generation to be 40 years. They base their reasoning on the following:

> *Num. 32:13* — "And the Lord's anger was kindled against Israel, and he made them wander in the wilderness *forty years*, until all the generation, that had done evil in the sight of the Lord, was consumed."

> *Ps. 95:10* — *"Forty years long was I grieved with this generation."*

> *Heb. 3:8-10* — "Harden not your hearts, as in the provocation, in the day of temptation in the wilderness: when your fathers tempted me, proved me, and *saw my works forty years*. Wherefore I was grieved with *that generation.*"

On this basis, the second coming of Jesus, when He comes

in power as Messiah-King, would have to occur not later than 1988 (1948 + 40). The revealing of Antichrist seven years previously, therefore, would place his exalted rise to power in the year 1981. That *might be* the year of "the Rapture."

JEWISH NEW YEAR

Dates in Scripture are based on the Hebrew calendar rather than the Roman or Gregorian calendars. Being a lunar calendar, the Hebrew (Jewish) sacred calendar begins on the new moon adjacent to the spring equinox.

In order to bring their lunar calendar into line with the Roman solar calendar, the Jews moved their New Year from Nisan 1 to Tishri 1, the first day of the seventh month of their sacred calendar. Their secular calendar starts with Rosh Hashana, the Jewish New Year, Tishri 1.

Their beginning of the year 1981, therefore, falls on Rosh Hashana, Tishri 1 (Feast of Trumpets), Sept. 11, 1980.

This presents an interesting combination.

The Balfour Declaration, "favoring the establishment of a national homeland in Palestine for the Jews," was signed Nov. 2, 1917. A prophetic span of 70 years from that date would be to Nov. 1987. Subtracting the seven years of Tribulation brings us to Rosh Hashana, Jewish New Year, the Feast of Trumpets of 1980.

Simultaneously, a 40-year span, a generation, from the rebirth of Israel as a nation on May 14, 1948 brings us to May 14, 1988. Subtracting the seven years of Tribulation then places us at May 1981. The Rosh Hashana — Feast of Trumpets — previous to that date brings us right back to Sept. 11, 1980.

Could this be the appointed time for the Rapture of the Church? Only God the Father knows for sure, but it has very high potential from a Bible standpoint.

THE LAST TRUMPET

"Behold, I shew you a mystery; We shall not all sleep (die), but we shall all be changed,

*"In a moment, in the twinkling of an eye, at the last
trump: for the trumpet shall sound, and the dead shall be
raised incorruptible, and we shall be changed"* (1 Corin.
15:51, 52).

Some people have greatly misunderstood the meaning of
the sounding of the last trumpet specified in 1 Corin. 15.

Only two trumpets are sounded here. One is to raise the
dead saints for the Rapture and the second trumpet is to
change the mortal bodies of the living saints into immortal
glorified bodies for the same event.

These two trumpets relate to the two silver trumpets used
in the days of the wilderness wanderings. When one trumpet
was sounded, it was for an assembly; but when a second alarm
was sounded it was for the moving of the camp.[3]

In the Bible, silver typifies redemption. *Praise God for the
two silver trumpets!* The first will raise the "dead in Christ"
and *the last trump* will herald our ascent to Glory.

"For this we say unto you by the word of the Lord, that
we which are alive and remain (at that moment) shall not
prevent (not precede) them which are asleep.

"For the Lord himself shall descend from heaven with
a shout, with the voice of the archangel, and with the
trump of God: and the dead in Christ shall rise first (at the
first trump):

"Then we which are alive and remain (at the last
trump) shall be caught up together with them in the
clouds to meet the Lord in the air, and so shall we ever be
with the Lord" (1 Thess. 4:15-17).

It is the two silver trumpets of Num. 10:2-6, the ones
used for the alarm to move the camp, that are alluded to here.

Some relate it to the seventh trumpet of Revelation, but
the seven trumpets sounded by the angels there have to do
with judgments on the people during the Tribulation period.
They do not at all relate to the Rapture of the Church. They
herald seven types of judgments on the earth, whereas we are
going to Glory. All of those judgments occur *after the Rapture*.

PROPHECY FULFILLMENTS

"The time of the end" — the generation that will see the return of the Lord in power and great glory — quite evidently had its beginning in 1948.

Israel

On May 14, 1948, Israel proclaimed its independence and became a nation again after more than 2,500 years of exile. This historic act undoubtedly started the countdown of "this generation."

The Ten Nation Empire

On June 8, 1948, Luxembourg, Belgium and The Netherlands signed the Benelux Agreement that became the foundation for the European Economic Community. The six-nation Common Market (EEC) came into being following the signing of the Treaty of Rome on March 25, 1957. Great Britain, Denmark and Ireland joined the Common Market Jan. 1, 1971, increasing its membership to nine nations.

On June 12, 1975, Greece asked the European Common Market to admit it as a full-fledged member "to coordinate democracy in Greece." Brendan Dillon, current chairman of the Committee of Permanent Representatives of Market Countries, called the request "a new event of great historical significance."[4]

May 29, 1979, Los Angeles Herald Examiner: "ATHENS, Greece — Greece became the 10th member of the European Common Market yesterday, culminating 22 years of efforts by Premier Constantine Caramanlis to join his country economically with Europe.

"A host of officials representing nine EEC members, including French President Valery Giscard d'Estaing, were on hand for glittering signing ceremonies in Athens' neo-classical Zappeion Congress Hall.

"Last to sign the treaty making Greece's membership in the EEC *official* was the 72-year-old Caramanlis . . .

"Greece's *active* membership is scheduled to start Jan. 1, 1981, after the 10 member parliaments ratify the agreement."

Watch for the 11th Nation!

An 11th nation is to join the Common Market 10.

> "Behold a fourth beast, dreadful and terrible . . . and it had ten horns.
>
> "I considered the horns, and, behold, there came up among them *another little horn*, before whom there were three of the first horns plucked up by the roots: and, behold, in this horn were eyes like the eyes of man, and a mouth speaking great things" (Dan. 7:7, 8).
>
> "And the ten horns out of this kingdom are ten kings that shall arise: and *another shall rise after them*; and he shall be diverse from the first, and he shall subdue three kings" (Dan. 7:24).

Thus we see that *after there are ten nations* in coalition, there is to arise *an 11th nation* and that the leader of this nation is to be "a man speaking great things" — the Antichrist.

There had to be the original 10 before there could be "*another* little horn." Greece signed the EEC treaty, and Greece's Parliament ratified it a few days later. The 11th nation and its infamous leader, "the king" of the Tribulation period, can come on the scene at any time even though Greece's *economic* participation with the EEC does not begin until Jan. 1, 1981.

Prophetically, therefore, as far as the 10-nation empire is concerned, only the entrance of the next, the 11th nation, awaits the prelude to the seven-year Tribulation.

Since three of the original ten are to be uprooted, and yet there are to remain ten nations throughout the Tribulation, it is preprequisite that there be 13 nations involved. It is interesting to note that three other nations already have applied for membership in the European Common Market — Austria, Spain and Portugal. Only after the revealing of the Antichrist king of the Tribulation period will it be known which three will be uprooted and which will be the replacements, but the potential is there TODAY.

Juan Carlos of Spain

"In *1948*, Juan Carlos of Spain began his training to become the king of Spain. For more than a quarter of a century he received specialized training under the watchful eye of military genius Gen. Francisco Franco. During that time he graduated from Spain's Naval Academy, its Airforce Academy and its famous Saragosa Military Academy, graduating third in a class of 271. For 27 years he waited as a "prince who shall come" (as of the prophecy of Dan. 9:26). When he was crowned king of Spain Nov. 22, 1975, he said, "Today represents *the beginning of a new stage* in the history of Spain."

It cannot be known at this time whether he will become the prophesied *king* of the end-time, but he does have more Bible-related qualifications than any other person in the political or military scene today, having been born in Rome and trained so extensively as a "prince who shall come." After his coronation he was honored by a Mass of the Holy Spirit, the highest honor of the Roman Catholic Church, in the 16th century Church of Los Jeronimose in Madrid. Present to pay their respects were representatives from 68 countries, the largest gathering of royalty and dignitaries in Spain's history, including three Common Market presidents and Vice President Nelson Rockefeller of the United States.

King Juan Carlos I has directed his course toward NATO and the European Common Market.

June 3, 1976, Los Angeles Times: "WASHINGTON (AP) — Spain's King Juan Carlos I began a bicentennial visit here with a pledge to end authoritarian rule in Spain by creating a system of 'authentic liberty.'

"In an address to a joint session of Congress, the tall, 38-year-old monarch said a chief goal of his regime is to ensure that every Spaniard 'has full scope for political participation without discrimination of any kind.'

"Juan Carlos, the first Spanish head of state to visit the United States, earlier received a red-carpet welcome at the White House, and President Ford endorsed the king's efforts to move Spain into the West European political mainstream . . . ."

Spain formally applied for Common Market membership July 28, 1977. In order for Spain to *qualify* for Common Market membership, it had to eliminate its fascism and adopt a democratic constitution.

Nov. 1, 1978, Los Angeles Times: "MADRID (AP) — Parliament voted overwhelming approval Tuesday of a new constitution guaranteeing human rights and providing for democracy under King Juan Carlos.

"The new constitution is Spain's 10th since 1808 and replaces the laws imposed during nearly four decades of dictatorship by Gen. Francisco Franco, who died Nov. 20, 1975. The 169 articles must now go before Spain's 21 million voters in a referendum that probably will be held Dec. 6."

Dec. 7, 1978, Los Angeles Times: "MADRID — Spanish voters Wednesday ratified a new democratic constitution, creating a parliamentary monarchy and closing the book on 40 years of fascism."

Aug. 1979, Spain 79: "By 285 votes in favor and two against, the Congress of Deputies passed a resolution presented by the parliamentary groups *supporting the entry of Spain into the European Economic Community . . .*"

"Among the political objectives of entry, (Foreign Minister) Sr. Oreja Aguirre mentioned the contribution to peace and *security of the zone.*"

Spain in Trilateral

Aug. 1979, Spain 79: "Carlos Ferrer Salat, President of the CEOE (Spanish Confederation of Employer's Organizations) and spokesman for the group of 13 Spaniards who have joined the Trilateral, declared at the 10th reunion of The Commission, which is made up of representatives from the United States, Japan and Europe, that he is convinced that 'Spain has vast possibilities of development and that the stability of countries in Southern Europe is essential for the Western World.' "

Rockefeller Favorable

Aug. 1979, Spain 79: "David Rockefeller, President of

Chase Manhattan Bank . . . was received by the King during his stay in Madrid.

" 'We have come to help finance the Spanish industry and, as far as possible, to co-operate with the Spanish government,' said the American banker."

$1,606,000,000 Surplus

Aug. 1979, Spain 79: "The monthly review 'Spanish Commercial Information,' published by the Ministry of Commerce and Tourism, gives the first official details on the closure of the current accounts balance for last year, which gave a surplus of 1,606 million dollars, in contrast to the deficit of 2,164.4 millions the year before."

Commentary

Spain's tremendous economic growth is seen by its advancing in one year from a 2 billion dollar deficit to a surplus of 1,606 million dollars. The first-line Bilderberg offer of co-financing for the government of Spain as well as for its industry also may be highly significant, as may be Spain's tie-in with the One-World-associated Trilateral Commission.

The overwhelming vote of Spain's Parliament to join the EEC places this country way out in front of other European nations that have made formal application to join the Common Market.

If Spain does become the 11th nation to join the existing 10-nation Roman Empire entity, whoever is king at that time will be given, according to the Bible, "a mouth speaking great things" (Dan. 7:8) and will be revealed as the infamous Antichrist of the Tribulation period (2 Thess. 2:8).

Could it be King Juan Carlos I, and could the year be 1980? Time alone will tell, but existing evidence indicates that it is *a distinct possibility*.

Regardless of the nation or the individual "king," Satan's chosen man soon will be revealed; but *not until after the Rapture of the church*. As of this writing, we still are in the closing days of the Church Age and have before us the Great Commission: "Go ye into all the world and preach the Gospel to every creature." May we be faithful witnesses to all the world that Jesus came to seek and to save that which was lost, and that now we can see that JESUS IS COMING SOON.

Juan Carlos and the Jews

June 4, 1976, Los Angeles Times: "WASHINGTON (AP) — Departing from a policy observed by Spanish heads of state for the past five centuries, Spain's King Juan Carlos I met with a delegation of American Jewish leaders.

"Former Supreme Court Justice Arthur Goldberg, who headed the 11-member delegation, said it was *the first meeting between a Spanish head of state and a Jewish delegation of any nationality since before 1492,* when Jews were expelled from Spain . . . .

"The meeting followed by six days an appearance by the king's wife, Queen Sophia, at a Madrid synagogue for a Jewish religious service, another milestone in the warming relations between the Spanish royalty and the Jewish community."

In another report, Queen Sophia explained, at a brief address at a dinner after the services at Madrid's synagogue, that she had asked to see the services to complement a seminar in humanities that she is taking at the University of Madrid. She said the seminar, which studies all religions, "is creating an ecumenical experience that will help promote an harmonious and united Spain."

Prophecy Commentary

The Bible prophecy significance in such reports as this is two-fold.

First of all, it shows that King Juan Carlos is extending his friendship to the Jewish people and is concerned about his relationship with the Jewish community and subsequently with Israel. It places him in a category that would be conducive to a guarantee of Israel's security such as the prophesied "covenant" of Dan. 9:27.

Secondly, the attendance of Queen Sophia at the meetings at the Jewish synagogue "creating an *ecumenical* experience" is a strong indication that the royal family's desire is to please all people, even to the extent of a study of *humanities,* which is a study of *all religions.* This tends toward the apostate ecumenical church system prophesied in Rev. 17 as being "BABYLON THE GREAT." It will constitute the false worldwide church system of the Tribulation period.

The first major move toward such a worldwide ecumenical church factor was the establishment of the World Council of Churches which held its first meeting, significantly, in Amsterdam *in 1948,* the same year Israel was reestablished as a nation after 2,500 years of subordination.

Yes, Bible prophecy *is* being fulfilled.

Juan Carlos — King of Jerusalem

I provided 16 pages of specific, documented information concerning the history, the attitudes and the statements of King Juan Carlos in my book *Get All Excited — Jesus Is Coming Soon.* His background is amazing. One item of note is the following:

Nov. 27, 1975, The Tablet, New York, NY: "JUAN CARLOS KING OF JERUSALEM: The swearing in of Prince Juan Carlos de Borbon as King of Spain automatically involved revival of an ancient title applied to Spanish monarchs, 'King of Jerusalem,' according to the Spanish consul general there. Count de Campo Rey said that the title, hereditary in Spanish royalty since the late Middle Ages, 'while empty and merely honorific,' today, was nevertheless 'extremely precious.' He said that 'Catholic Kings' of Spain had been recognized by Popes and Muslim rulers for centuries as 'protectors of Catholic Holy Land interests.' "

Such a relevant title might be just coincidental, *but is it?* With Spain so rapidly approaching the status of *the 11th nation,* and having such a highly trained military king holding such a significant title, one cannot but wonder, "IS THIS THE 'KING' OF THE TRIBULATION?"

Covenant Conditions

In order for the nations of Western Europe to select a

military leader and then be willing to follow him into a war primarily to defend the nation of Israel, that group of nations would need to be already inclined in that direction.

On June 9-11, 1979, the first multinational election in history was held in the Common Market countries of Western Europe.

June 12, 1979, Los Angeles Times: "Final returns in Europe's first multinational election gave a coalition of Liberals, Christian Democrats and British Conservatives a working majority in the European Parliament of the Common Market. The center-right bloc won 207 seats in the 410-member Parliament. Socialist won 111 seats, and Communists 42 — 24 from Italy and 18 from France. The remaining seats will be held by Progressive Democrats and other small and diverse factions from across Europe."

The first assembly of the newly elected European Parliament met in the European Palace at Strasbourg, France, on July 17. Its first order of business was to select a president to preside over the congress. Here is the interesting result of that parliamentary election:

July 18, 1979, Los Angeles Times: "STRAUSBOURG, France (AP) — The European Parliament, history's first directly elected multinational assembly, opened its inaugural session Tuesday and elected as its first president Simone Veil, a Jewish Frenchwoman who survived the Auschwitz death camp.

"Before the vote, Mrs. Veil — dressed as usual in a long-sleeved dress that covers the number 78651 tatooed on her arm by the Nazis — sat inconspicuously in a back row.

"Her election provided a poignant moment in Europe's quest to bury the memory of Hitler and become united.

"It was a measure of how far Europe had evolved democratically from the Hitler years. Never was Mrs. Veil's sex, religion or tragic past a factor in her ascent to high European office.

"Mrs. Veil, a mother of three, served as health minister in France until being elected to the Parliament of the nine Common Market nations June 10."

Since any selection of a common king or leader of Western

Europe would most likely be made by the European Parliament, and since the prophesied king who is to be chosen is to almost immediately make a covenant to guarantee Israel's security for seven years (Dan. 9:27), it is highly significant that the first elected president of the European Parliament is a Jewess that lived through the Auschwitz ordeal. Most certainly she would favor such a king!

Everything seems to be pointing to the soon acclamation of a leader for the 10-nation empire of "the time of the end." Tribulation is coming.

You need to know the Lord as Savior, *or* you might be one of those who will have to go through that terrible time called the Tribulation. Accept Christ today — NOW — so you will not be among *Those Who Remain*.

Footnotes

[1] Dan. 9:24
[2] Dan. 9:26
[3] Num. 10:2
[4] Los Angeles Times, June 13, 1975

Portion of Veteran's Administration Hospital,
Los Angeles County, Feb. 9, 1971.

CHAPTER 10

THE JUPITER EFFECT

Scientists have been studying the effect of the planets on each other and on the sun.

One of the most notable stellar scientists is Dr. John Gribbin who received his doctorate in astro-physics at Cambridge University in England and is an editor of *Nature*, an international journal of science published in London.

Another is Dr. Steven Plagemann, a physics major at the University of California at Berkeley. He received his doctorate in 1971 at Cambridge university and worked at the Institute of Theoretical Astronomy under the eminent astronomer Sir Fred Hoyle. Dr. Plagemann has worked on special projects for the U.S. Geological Survey and in a NASA study of the upper atmosphere phenomena as gathered by Earth satellite. He lives in Washington D.C.

Dr. Gribbin and Dr. Plagemann combined their efforts, knowledge and findings in a study of the planets in relation to the sun and the Earth, revealed by the space exploration and satellite program of the last decade. Their findings were printed in a highly technical scientific book called *The Jupiter Effect*. The following summary information is from that book.

Basic Information

Galileo began recording sunspot activity in 1610, and records have been kept almost continuously ever since that date. Measurements of the speed and intensity of solar winds by Earth satellites and by scientific instruments placed on the moon by our astronauts has verified that solar storms send cosmic winds throughout our solar system, affecting the upper atmosphere of the Earth. These in turn can affect the rate of the Earth's spin. Even a slight change of that rate of spin tends to cause earthquakes.

Many documented reports in *The Jupiter Effect* verify the

interrelationship of the sun and the planets. The ratio is determined by the relative positions of the nine planets each to the other and to the sun.

When Earth and Venus are in conjunction (on the same side of the sun) or in opposition (on the opposite sides of the sun), they combine to raise a total tide on the sun about 50 per cent greater than the largest tide ever raised by the planet Jupiter. When Earth, Venus and Jupiter are all aligned, their combined tidal effects add together on the sun's surface. The relation between sunspot activity and these tidal influences is beyond question. The predictions of tidal heights are exact.

At times between 1977 and 1982 all the planets of our solar system will be aligned on the same side of the sun. This happens every 179 years. But the unusual factor *this* time is that the nine planets will be not only on one side of the sun within 180 degrees of each other, *they will be in almost a straight line*. This will greatly increase the gravitational pull of the planets on the surface of the sun. As a result, there will be very great sunspot activity, causing huge solar storms.

The cosmic rays emitted by these storms will produce solar winds so extreme that they are sure to effect the rate of the Earth's spin. The greater change, the heavier jolt; and some scientists fear that planet Earth will face one of the greatest disasters ever known. Most all agree that there will be many earthquakes and that one or more will be extreme. Of one thing we can be absolutely sure: the unusual planetary alignment is definitely approaching, and it *will* effect the activity of the sun.

The Alignment

When Jupiter aligns with Mars, in the early months of 1982, the sun's activity will be at a peak; streams of charged particles will flow out past the planets, including Earth, and there will be a profound effect on the overall cosmic circulation and on the weather patterns.

Finally, the last link in the chain, movements of large masses of the atmosphere will agitate regions of the globe. Within two years of 1982 there will be a major disaster. At the end point of the chain, directly causing this disaster, is that rare line-up of the planets in our solar system. By disturbing the equilibrium of the sun, which in turn disturbs the whole Earth, THE PLANETS CAN AND WILL TRIGGER EARTHQUAKES.

"There is no question about the implication: in 1982-1984 when . . . Jupiter aligns with Mars and with the other seven planets of the solar system, Los Angeles, on the San Andreas fault, will be destroyed" (The Jupiter Effect, pg. 116).

Many earthquakes will occur, but the heaviest quake will be a disastrous one.

Prophecies About Earthquakes

The significance of *The Jupiter Effect* is that the projections of the book fit perfectly with Bible prophecy. Jesus said that one of the signs of His return would be "earthquakes in many places" (Matt. 24:7).

I have noticed a pronounced increase in the number of earthquakes being reported in the news periodicals. The following is a summary of just those recorded in our local papers in 1975:

Jan. 24, 1975: "A series of 297 earthquakes has been recorded in southern Japan in the last three days, touching off fears a major eruption may be forthcoming, the Meteorological Agency said today."

Jan. 28, 1975: "More than 1,000 mild to moderate earthquakes have shaken Southern California in the past six days. Most of the earthquakes have been in the desert region near the Mexican border. But the latest rolled through San Fernando Valley late Monday night . . . The most active days were Saturday and Sunday, with more than 400 quakes a day."

March 14, 1975: "A violent and prolonged earthquake struck central Chile, toppling walls in the provincial capital of La Serena . . . It caused tall buildings to sway in Santiago."

March 14, 1975: "The Institute of Seismology reported today that a 'relatively powerful' tremor occurred in the Pacific several hours after an earthquake killed two people in Chile. The Institute located it between the New Hebrides and Loyalty Islands in the Western Pacific. It measured 6.9 on the Richter scale, while the quake in Chili registered 7.."

March 27, 1975: "A strong earthquake hit northern Turkey on both sides of the Strait of the Dardenelles early today. . . . Istanbul's Kandilli Observatory said the quake registered 5.6 on the Richter scale. It was 'intense enough to result in devastation at the origin' it said."

March 28, 1975: "SALT LAKE CITY — The strongest earthquake in the continental United States since the deadly Southern California tremor of 1971 struck in desolate desert country along the Utah-Idaho line Thursday night, causing minor damage. The quake swayed buildings in downtown Salt Lake City, broke windows and crumbled plaster in the small towns of Malad, Idaho, and Snowville, Utah, and was felt throughout much of northern Utah, southeastern Idaho and southwestern Wyoming . . . The National Earthquake Information Center at Golden, Colorado said the tremor measured 6.3 on the Richter scale."

April 6, 1975: "An earthquake struck a triangle of Western Venezuelan cities early Saturday, shattering one small town, killing two and injuring scores of other persons . . . The Cajigal Observatory in Caracas reported its intensity as reaching 5.3 on the Richter scale. The U.S. Geological Survey in Washington registered the quake as slightly sharper — 6.3 on the Richter scale . . . The quake was also felt in Caracas as well as other cities in central and western Venezuela."

May 13, 1975: "A moderate earthquake rumbled through a strip of Southern California more than 100 miles long Monday evening, including the Los Angeles area, but apparently did no significant damage. A quake with the magnitude of 4.5 on the Richter scale struck the area and was felt from Bakersfield to the coast of Santa Barbara County and south through downtown Los Angeles, Santa Monica, the San Fernando Valley and elsewhere in the Los Angeles area."

May 27, 1975: "THE WORLD'S STRONGEST EARTHQUAKE IN RECENT YEARS hit the Atlantic Ocean floor between the Azores and the Iberian Peninsula Monday. The quake was most strongly felt in the Madeira Islands, 500 miles southwest of Lisbon. Marcus Baath, director of the Seismological Institute in Uppsala, Sweden, said the quake registered 7.9 on the Richter scale."

June 8, 1975: "FORTUNA, CALIF. — Damage reports are

pouring in as residents on the southern tip of Humboldt Bay clean up Saturday after the worst earthquake to hit this area in two decades. The jolt, registering 5.4 on the Richter scale, heaved people out of bed and toppled chimneys."

June 15, 1975: "A violent earthquake shook central Chili Saturday. It temporarily blacked out Santiago and other cities, officials said. The U.S. Geological Survey in Washington said the tremor occurred about 60 miles under the Earth's surface. Amid screams of panic, some of the fruit and vegetable vendors began to pray. 'This is about the only time most of them remember God,' one of the fruit stand owners said."

June 15, 1975: "Several earthquakes shook Japan early today . . . One tremor was felt in Tokyo itself and north and east of the Japanese capital. Its epicenter was believed to be in the Pacific Ocean off Honshu, Japan's main island. The Meteorological Agency said two earthquakes were also recorded in the eastern part of Hokkaido."

June 21, 1975: "A swarm of 20 earthquakes shook this Imperial Valley community within a 29-hour period, the Caltech Seismological Laboratory reported Friday . . . The quake activity began at 12:02 p.m. Thursday with a tremor of 3.5 on the Richter scale, followed at 9:14 p.m. with a 3.9 tremor and a 4.2 quake at 10:48 p.m. On Friday, there were quakes of 4.1 on the scale at 3:15 p.m. and 3.2 at 3:49 p.m. Fifteen other quakes were recorded at Caltech in Pasadena, according to spokesman Graham Berry."

August 2, 1975: "OROVILLE (UPI) — A series of earthquakes, some centered just five miles from the nation's tallest earthfilled dam, rolled from north to south through California Friday. The strongest quake, in the northern part of the state, shook an area 300 miles long and 175 miles wide, registered 6.1 on the Richter scale and caused several injuries, one reportedly serious. It was felt as far away as Fresno and Carson City, Nev., and lasted about a minute.

"Only hours later, a moderate quake centered in the mountains 15 to 20 miles south of Palm Springs, jarred Southern California and was felt over a 130-mile area as far as Los Angeles and San Diego County, with a magnitude of 4.9 on the Richter scale."

Sept. 14, 1975: "OROVILLE (AP) — Earthquakes have sunk the Oroville area about six inches in relation to the Sierras. Another quake in the area is a 'reasonable probability,' a federal report said Saturday."

Oct. 12, 1975: "WASHINGTON (AP) — A major earthquake struck the New Hebrides Islands region in the southwest Pacific Ocean Saturday and another tremor rocked the ocean floor off Acapulco in the eastern Pacific. The U.S. Geological Survey reported the New Hebrides earthquake occurred about 10:36 a.m. EDT and registered about 7.8 on the Richter scale, according to the survey's Earthquake Information Center . . . Waverly Person of the center in Golden, Colorado, said an earthquake with a magnitude of 7.2 occurred in the same area Oct. 6. Several lesser tremors were reported in southern Mexico the same day. Yet another quake occurred 3,000 miles north of Chili on Oct. 7, possibly in the Pacific near Central America . . ."

Oct. 7, 1975: "A series of earth tremors toppled about 300 houses and injured dozens of people in the Mexican state of Chiapas, about 450 miles south of Mexico City, authorities reported . . . The strongest shock registered 5.5 on the Richter scale."

Oct. 31, 1975: "A major earthquake rocked sparsely populated parts of the Philippines today. The National Earthquake Information Center in Golden, Colo., and the U.S. Geological Survey in Washington, D.C., reported the quake occurred at 3:28 p.m. EST and registered 7.3 on the Richter scale. A 7 reading is considered a 'major' quake capable of causing widespread heavy damage."

Nov. 16:1975: "An earthquake rattled the western and central areas of Mexico, shattering windows and cracking walls . . . Thousands of panic-stricken people in towns of Michoacan state of the Pacific coast fled into the streets or sought shelter under beds, desks and furniture."

Nov. 30, 1975: "THE STRONGEST EARTHQUAKE TO HIT THE ISLANDS IN 100 YEARS jolted Hawaii Saturday, triggering a tidal wave and a volcanic eruption. One man was killed, another missing and 34 persons were taken to island hospitals with injuries, officials said.

"The earthquake came in two big shocks — the first at 3:30

a.m., registered 5.5 on the Richter scale, and the second, about an hour later, registered 7.2. There were sharp after-shocks throughout the morning . . .

"Residents of coastal areas were evacuated and police sealed off downtown Hilo, the island's largest city, with 26,000 residents, to prevent looting. Glass and Christmas decorations were scattered in the streets . . ."

Dec. 31, 1975: PATRAS, Greece (AP) — An earthquake jolted western Greece today, causing heavy damage to towns and villages. The villages of Ano and Kato Makrinou were said to be leveled. About 1,500 persons live in these two villages. Hundreds of homes were reported damaged in other nearby villages, leaving several thousand persons homeless. Power lines collapsed, cutting off regular communications, but police said they were in radio contact with the worst-hit area. Police said the quake registered 5.8 on the Richter scale."

Most assuredly, earthquakes already have been happening "in many places." The reports I documented here are just the ones I happened to notice and clip from the daily papers. Seismology reports would show thousands more in many locations and in all variations of intensity. They *are* happening!

Tragic earthquakes struck Guatemala early in 1976. Major jolts came on Feb. 4, 1976 and were followed by many aftershocks that destroyed huge areas. The official death count was 22,084, with 74, 105 injured and well over one million people homeless.

242,000 Killed in China Quake

The most disastrous earthquake to date, however, was the one that struck a heavily populated area in China July 28, 1976. Not until November of 1979 was any official information available about this strongest of earthquakes recorded on Earth preliminary to the coming "parade of the planets." Here is the brief announcement:

Nov. 24, 1979, The Register, Orange Co., New York Times News Service: "PEKING — The earthquake that hit Tang-shan in Red China *in 1976* killed 242,000 people and seriously injured 164,000, Red China said Friday, the first time it has released any estimate of the extent of the disaster.

"The earthquake measured 7.8 on the Richter scale and struck a heavily populated triangular area bounded by Tangshan, Peking and the port city of Tianjin. Tangshan itself, an industrial and coalmining city of 1 million people was virtually flattened."

And the scientific prediction is that there are many more earthquakes to come within the next few years.

The Warning Words of Jesus

Jesus may have had this "parade of the planets" in mind when He declared in Luke 21:25-27:

> **"And there shall be signs in the sun, and in the moon, and in the stars; and upon the earth distress of nations, with perplexity; the sea and the waves roaring; men's hearts failing them for fear, and for looking after those things which are coming on the earth: FOR THE POWERS OF HEAVEN SHALL BE SHAKEN.**
>
> **"And** *then* **shall they see the Son of man coming in a cloud with power and great glory."**

After the *last* great earthquake has struck, Jesus will descend in a cloud, "And His feet shall stand in that day upon the Mount of Olives, which is before Jerusalem on the east."[4] The time for His long-awaited reign of PEACE will have come, for the Tribulation period will have ended. The last great earthquake will have happened.

Footnotes

[1] Read "The Year of Beginnings: 1948," the 20-page Chapter 22 in my book *World War III and the Destiny of America.*

[2] Read "The Man With the Potential," a 16-page chapter in my book *Get All Excited — Jesus Is Coming Soon.*

[3] *LOS ANGELES TIMES*, June 13, 1975.

[4] Zech. 14:4

CHAPTER 11

WORLD WAR III
AND ITS RESULTS

When World War III happens, it will be a horrible holocaust. The U.S.A. and Western European powers will blast the Soviet Union and the U.S.S.R. will fire thousands of nuclear missiles at the West. It will be all-out fury, fulfilling the prophecy of Ezek. 39:8 —

> *"Behold, it is come and it is done, saith the Lord God, this is the day whereof I have spoken."*

Our land-based ICBMs, Polaris and Poseidon submarine-launched missiles, air-launched cruise missiles and nuclear bombs will bring such devastation on our enemies that the prophecy of Ezek. 39:6 likewise will be fulfilled:

> *"And I will send a fire on Magog (Russia)"*

Isaiah, Ezekiel and Daniel record that the Arab nations will flee in terror when they see the destruction and realize that five-sixths of Russia's mighty armies have fallen "on the mountains of Israel."[1]

Israel will be delivered and will no longer be hampered by Arab threats. The Jews will build a Temple on Mt. Moriah in East Jerusalem and will reinstate animal sacrifices.

America? It will be so severely damaged in the nuclear exchange that it no longer will be a superpower. *But it will survive as a nation.*

A leader from Western Europe will claim the military victory over the Russians and Arabs and will establish himself as the head of a Revived Roman Empire. He will be the Antichrist.

U.S. Plans for Survival

The United States government has made extensive plans

for the survival of THOSE WHO REMAIN after World War III. The details of several of these plans and provisions have been documented in this book, and the prospects are not pleasant.

God's Plan for Survival

The Lord God is fully aware of the situation, however, and has made much better plans and provisions for those who will believe His Word and who will trust in His Son, the Lord Jesus Christ.

The Lord is going to remove His believing Church from the Earth *before* the holocaust of World War III and the harsh events to follow.

> **"For the Lord himself shall descend from heaven with a shout, with the voice of the archangel, and with the trump of God: and the dead in Christ shall rise first: then we who are alive and remain shall be caught up together with them in the clouds, to meet the Lord in the air: and so shall we ever be with the Lord" (I Thess. 4:16, 17).**

The full plan of deliverance and salvation has been outlined. Also a warning to all who reject God's provision.

The Future for Those Who Remain

After believing Christians are removed from Earth, the Gospel of the Kingdom will be preached by 144,000 specially chosen Jewish people, whom God's angel will seal for protection during the first half of the Tribulation period; their ministry will last three-and-one-half years; and their message will be that Christ is coming soon as the Jewish Messiah, Prince of Peace and King of Kings. Millions will believe their God-given message of salvation by faith in Christ, but the Antichrist will kill those whom he can reach. An end-time false church system will do likewise.

The result will be that all who believe in Christ during the first half of the Tribulation will be slain.

Their lives on Earth will be cut short, but God will have great provision for them in Heaven. In the Revelation, John wrote:

"These are they which came out of great tribulation, and have washed their robes, and made them white in the blood of the Lamb. Therefore are they before the throne of God, and serve him day and night in his temple: and he that sitteth on the throne shall dwell among them.

"They shall hunger no more, neither thirst any more; neither shall the sun light on them, nor any heat. For the Lamb (Jesus Christ) which is in the midst of the throne shall feed them, and shall lead them unto living fountains of waters: *and God shall wipe away all tears from their eyes*" (Rev. 7:14-17).

Satan's Plans

The Tribulation period will last just seven years. The Antichrist will be in authority for the full time, but *in the middle of Daniel's week of years* — after 3½ years — he will receive a fatal head wound (Rev. 13:3-5), then come back to life. When he does he will be indwelt by Satan, for God's angels will have thrown that old devil out of heaven by that time. Because Satan is a spirit being, he must have a body to be seen on Earth. Therefore, he will take over the body of the Antichrist king.

When Satan enters the body of the Antichrist, he will enter the Jewish temple in Jerusalem , announce that he is God and demand to be worshipped as God (II Thess. 2:4).

That is when his false prophet will make an image of Antichrist and require all people to worship it or die. Those who worship the devil, or his image, will receive a special "mark of the beast" or the number of his name, which will be 666. No one will be able to buy or sell (to live) without the identification mark.

These things have been explained in this book.

At the end of the seven-year Tribulation, following a final great earthquake — one worse than any the world has ever seen, the Lord Jesus Christ will come in all His power and great glory as KING OF KINGS and LORD OF LORDS. He will defeat and destroy the Antichrist and his false prophet and will set up a dominion of perfect peace on Earth. God's plan will have been fulfilled.

I have given the warnings.

The way of salvation and deliverance has been made plain. The choice is up to you — and to THOSE WHO REMAIN.

Footnotes

[1]Ezekiel 39:1-5

CONCLUSION

Since all the nations mentioned in the Bible as participants in the great war over Israel at the beginning of the Tribulation period, the one we call World War III, are now feverishly preparing for that precise war, the time has to be at hand.

The one event scheduled by the Lord to take place *before* World War III is *"the rapture of the church."* How soon? Only the Lord knows the moment, but all the signs point to the immediate future.

If the Feast of Trumpets of 1980 is the time when the born again Christians will hear "a shout, the voice of the archangel and the trump of God," would YOU be ready or would you be among THOSE WHO REMAIN?

CHRONOLOGY OF MIDDLE EAST CRISIS

1882

First group of Jewish colonists settle in Palestine. The Holy Land is part of the Ottoman Empire (Turkey) at this time.

1896

Publication of Theodor Herzl's book, *The Jewish State*, advocating a Jewish nation in a Jewish national land: "We shall live at last as free men on our own soil . . ."

1897

Aug. 29—Opening of the first Zionist Congress in Basle, Switzerland. (The first time in more than 1,800 years a representative body of the Jewish people was met together openly to discuss ways and means for the return to Zion.)

1914

Nov. 2-5—The Allies (England, France, Russia) declare war on the Ottoman Empire.

1917

Oct. 31—British forces, under General Allenby, begin advance into Palestine from Egypt. By October 1918, British drive through Palestine deep into Syria.

Nov. 2—Balfour Declaration — British government pledges "the establishment in Palestine of a national home for the Jewish people."

1918

March—Zionist Commission sent to Palestine by the British government to plan and prepare for the execution of the Balfour Declaration.

Oct. 30—Allies conclude armistice with the Turks. Turkish territory placed at the disposal of the Allies.

1920

April 25—Iraq mandated to Great Britain.

Sept. 1—Lebanon and Syria mandated to France.

1922

July 24—League of Nations approves French mandate for Syria and British mandate for Palestine and Trans-Jordan.

1926

Jan. 8—Ibn Saud proclaimed King of the Hejaz and Sultan of Nejd (later Saudi Arabia).

1929

Aug.—Palestinian Arabs open large scale attacks on Jewish settlers. Riots and terror continue through 1930's and '40's until Israeli independence.

1932

Oct. 3—Iraq becomes independent.

1943

Nov. 22—Lebanon attains independence from France. French withdrawal completed by December 1946.

1944

Jan. 1—Syria becomes independent on French relinquishment of mandate powers.

1945

Mar. 22—Syria, Lebanon, Iraq, Saudi Arabia, Egypt, Trans-Jordan and Yemen form the Arab League to oppose the establishment of a State of Israel.

1946

Mar. 22—Trans-Jordan attains full independence with the end of British mandate.

1947

Nov. 29—The United Nations votes to partition Palestine into Jewish and Arab states. Jews approve plan but it is rejected by the Arabs.

1948

May 14-15—British end the Palestine mandate. The state of Israel is proclaimed. Egypt, Trans-Jordan, Syria, Iraq, Lebanon and Saudi Arabia attack Israel.

Sept. 25—An Arab government claiming *all* of Palestine set up in Gaza by approval of the Arab League. This "government," rejected by King Abdullah of Trans-Jordan, never became functional.

Dec. 20—King Abdullah appoints Sheik Hussan Meddin Jarallah as Mufti (Moslem ruler) in Jerusalem.

1949

Feb. 24-July 20—Unsuccessful Arab invasion of Israel is ultimately terminated by a series of armistice agreements.

April 26—Trans-Jordan, having conquered West Bank lands, west of the Jordan River, drops name of Trans-Jordan in favor of constitutional name Hashemite Kingdom of Jordan.

April 26—All Arabs in the West Bank (including East Jerusalem) become citizens of Jordan, an action never approved by nor accepted by the Arab League.

1950

April 24—Jordan annexes that part of Palestine which had remained under Jordanian control after the armistice agreement.

1951

July 20—King Abdullah of Jordan is assassinated and is succeeded by his son, Talal. Talal declared unfit to rule and is succeeded by his son, Hussein, in 1953.

1956

July 26—Egypt's President Gamal Abdel Nasser nationalizes Suez Canal, blocks Strait of Tiran, Israel's only access to Red Sea.

Oct. 29—Israel invades Sinai. France and Britain join attack. Israeli army captures Gaza Strip, occupies most of peninsula east of Suez Canal.

1957

March—Under joint U.S.-Soviet pressure, Israeli troops withdraw from occupied Egyptian territory. A 4,500-man U.N. force is stationed at tip of Sinai Peninsula to ensure free passage through Strait of Tiran.

1958

May-July—Civil War erupts in Lebanon. U.S. forces called in by Lebanese president. British troops sent to Jordan.

1960

Aug. 16—Cyprus attains independence after five years of Greek Cypriot agitation.

1961

Sept. 28—Syrian opposition to Nasser's nationalization policies results in Syria's withdrawal from the United Arab Republic, leaving Egypt and Syria as separate Arab states.

1963

Dec. 21—Fighting breaks out between Greek and Turkish communities on Cyprus.

1966

Feb. 23—Extreme anti-Israel group overthrows moderate Syrian government. Terrorists raid Israeli border areas during following months.

1967

May 18—Nasser demands withdrawal of U.N. forces from the Sinai. U.N. complies and Egyptian troops mobilize to occupy the area.

May 22—Nasser announces Egyptian blockade of Strait of Tiran against Israeli shipping.

June 5-10—Israel wins lightning victory in six days over Egypt, Syria and Jordan, captures over $1 billion in Russian-Arab armaments. Israeli army seizes most of Sinai Peninsula, the Jordanian sector of Jerusalem and all the West Bank region plus the Golan Heights.

June 12—Israeli Premier Levi Eshkol declares Israel will retain control of occupied territories.

Nov. 22—U.N. Security Council adopts resolution calling for peace in Mideast based on withdrawal of Israeli troops from occupied territories.

1968-73

Many terrorist attacks on Israel by Palestinian Arabs operating from neighboring Arab states, more recently from Lebanon.

1973

Oct. 6—Egypt and Syria attack Israel on Yom Kippur, the Jewish Day of Atonement. After heavy losses, Israel defeated both

Arab states despite Arab assistance from six other Arab League
nations. The U.N. ordered a cease-fire on Oct. 22 and another
Oct. 24. Israel observed the latter. The Soviet Union and the
U.S.A. had both ordered full military alert of their strategic
armed services. After the cease-fire, U.S. Secretary of State
Henry A. Kissinger negotiated for and obtained the first actual
peace agreement ever signed between Israel and any Arab
state: the Egyptian-Israeli agreement signed in September
1975.

1974

Oct. 29—20-nation Arab League gives the Palestine Liberation
Organization (PLO) full recognition as the "sole legitimate
representative of the Palestinian people." Hussein agrees.

Nov. 22—U.N. General Assembly overwhelmingly endorses permanent observer status for the PLO.

1975

June 11—President Assad of Syria and King Hussein of Jordan agree
to unite their military forces in any war with Israel, reviving
the old Arab eastern front against Israel.

1976

Civil War in Lebanon has resulted in the overthrow of the Christian
majority rule and a takeover by Arab control, be it in conjunction with Syria, the Arab League or other Arab leaders. This
means higher potential for a combined Arab thrust against
Israel when the crucial time comes. And all the Arab factions
receive arms supplies and advice from officials in the Kremlin.
Russian backed Arabs now face Israel "from the north parts."

1977

March—Palestine National Council reaffirms endorsement of PLO's
1968 Covenant. It calls for dismantling of the State of Israel.

April 5-8—Yasser Arafat of the PLO meets Soviet party chief Leonid
I. Brezhnev for first time. Brezhnev pledges Russian support
for an independent Palestinian state.

Oct. 16—U.N. reports US and USSR have 12,000 nuclear warheads
deployed for war, having "combined explosive power . . .
equivalent to 1.3 Hiroshima-size bombs plus many smaller tactical nuclear weapons equaling another 50,000 Hiroshima-size
atom bombs." Arms race costing $350 billion annually accord-
ing to report.

Nov. 17—Pres. Sadat's historic visit to Jerusalem. First de facto
Arab recognition of State of Israel.

Dec.—Arab nations unite against Egyptian peace effort. Egypt
ousted from Arab League participation.

1978

Immense buildup of Soviet armaments on land, sea and in strategic
aircraft. Soviet defense budget estimated at $150 billion.

June—Prime Minister Bulent Ecivit of Turkey signs "political document" pledging "good relations" with the Soviet Union.

Aug.—Arab nations reportedly have received $43 billion in military aid from Soviets since 1973.

1979

March 26—Carter, Begin and Sadat sign peace agreement in Washington D.C. ending 30 years of war between Egypt and Israel.

May 28—Greece signs treaty to become 10th member of European Community.

June 7-10—Common Market countries elect first universal European Parliament.

July 17—Jewess Simone Veil of France elected as first President of European Community.

July—Pres. Assad of Syria and Yasser Arafat of PLO both secure more advanced arms from Soviets. Col. Kadaffi of Libya reportedly receives balance of $12 billion in armaments from Soviets.

August—Spain joins EFTA and its Cortez (parliament) votes also to unite with European Community.

Turkey grants full diplomatic status to PLO.

Sept. 7—Pres. Carter announces final approval of MX intercontinental ballistic missile system.

Oct. 25—South Yemen signs 20-year treaty of friendship with Moscow.

Nov. 4—Militants seize U.S. Embassy in Tehran, Iran. Hostages held by "students."

Dec. 25—Soviet army invades Afghanistan.

1980

Jan. 17—Rejectionist Arab leaders call Soviet Union "true friend of Arabs and Muslims."

Jan. 23—Israel returns major portion of Sinai to Egypt. Little or no progress in Palestine autonomy talks.

Jan. 23—Pres. Carter puts stiff restrictions on Soviet trade, proclaims Persian Gulf region within "the vital interests of the United States" and pledges military protection, increases U.S. defense budget.

Polarization of superpowers and their respective allies. Western powers stiffen opposition to Soviets and militant Muslims.

Jan. (14), 1980 News and World Report: "Pentagon officials just back from a trip to European capitals were surprised to discover that *a major war involving Russia — considered unthinkable only a year ago — is now seen as a possibility in the 1980s.*"

PREPARE TO MEET THY GOD!

BIBLE CHART

OF THE TRIBULATION PERIOD

Many have asked that I personally chart the order of events of the Church Age and the Tribulation period. I have this chart for you now.

Covering major events from the Cross to the New Heaven and New Earth, this chart shows in detail a picture of the events from this moment until the return of Christ in power at the close of the Tribulation (and beyond). Events in Heaven and on Earth are listed, verified by many Bible references. This chart information will help you debunk many false ideas being promoted today.

Too large to be included in the book *Those Who Remain,* it is sold separately. Black & White — $1.00; Multicolor — $4.00.

Cassettes by Dr. Charles R. Taylor

REVELATION TAUGHT IN CHRONOLOGICAL ORDER

A complete study of Revelation coordinated with the Old Testament prophecies and the teachings of Christ as taught in chronological arrangement on 215 radio broadcasts. Most comprehensive study available anywhere.
Any 10 cassettes (50 programs) — $29.95.
Complete series of 215 broadcasts on 43 cassettes — $119.95.

INSTRUCTIONS FOR THOSE WHO REMAIN (cassette)

This message of warning tells of events that will happen *after the rapture.* It gives instruction for physical survival and for spiritual salvation during the Tribulation period. Very informative, and with a soul-winning message. 1½ hour — $4.95.

INSTRUCCIONES PARA LOS QUE SE QUEDEN

Spanish narration of the same message as translated and narrated by Rev. Terry Moran. 60 minutes — $4.00.

HOW TO ORDER BOOKS OR CASSETTES

Send cash, check or money order to

TODAY IN BIBLE PROPHECY, INC.
P.O. Box 2500
Orange, CA 92669

20% discount for 12 or more books to one address.

REGULAR TRADE DISCOUNT FOR ALL BOOKSTORES